Judith Rodin
President, The Rockefeller Foundation

Margot Brandenburg

THE
PWER
OF
IMPACT
INVESTING

Putting Markets to Work for
Profit and Global Good

DIGITAL PRESS
Philadelphia

Published by Wharton Digital Press
The Wharton School
University of Pennsylvania
3620 Locust Walk
2000 Steinberg Hall–Dietrich Hall
Philadelphia, PA 19104
Email: whartondigitalpress@wharton.upenn.edu
Website: wdp.wharton.upenn.edu

Ebook ISBN: 978-1-61363-035-8
Paperback ISBN: 978-1-61363-036-5

10 9 8 7 6 5 4 3 2

Please contact Wharton Digital Press for special discounts on bulk purchases
of ebooks and paperbacks: whartondigitalpress@wharton.upenn.edu.

Contents

Introduction

For nearly 30 years, Ron Cordes made his living, and a comfortable one at that, in finance. He and his partners built an investment services firm with $9 billion in assets, 400 employees, and offices across the country. In 2006 he sold the business to a large investment firm for $230 million. But as he reached his fifties, he began searching for something to fill the next chapter in his life.

He and his wife, Marty, set up a family foundation (and were later joined by their daughter, Stephanie), but they found the prospect of granting money, in a way that could bring about real change, daunting. With modest foundation funds, Cordes was struggling to come up with grant-making strategies that would have a lasting impact.

He decided he needed to see the effect of poverty for himself. On his first trip to Africa, he visited a village in Uganda five hours east of the nation's capital, Kampala. With the images of starving children so often seen on television fresh in his brain, he expected to be greeted by scenes of hopelessness and despair. Instead, he met a group of women whose entrepreneurial spirit inspired him to transform his approach to giving.

The women, widows who had lost their husbands in the Ugandan civil war, were recipients of small loans given out by a microfinance program Cordes's foundation had funded. With the loans, the women had started raising chickens, selling clothing, and running a café. Rather than relying on Western aid, the women explained, they wanted to establish livelihoods and support their children on their own.

"That was a powerful moment for me," Cordes said in a TEDx talk he gave in 2011.[1] "It changed my whole perception of the way I was looking at the problem of poverty—I was looking at the poor as victims who needed us to create solutions for them instead of folks that were entirely capable of being the creators of their own solutions, if they were given just a hand up."

Cordes also realized he could best tackle social and environmental challenges as he had once approached his entrepreneurship: by seeking solutions that would be self-sustaining and replicable and that could be rapidly expanded. Rather than launch his own initiatives, he saw that more could be achieved by putting funds into the innovative social enterprises being developed by others. As a result, since 2007, Cordes has dedicated much of his foundation's financial resources to impact investments alongside its philanthropy.

Put simply, impact investments are intended to deliver both financial returns and social and environmental benefits. Although investing directly in socially motivated companies or projects, as Cordes has done, might require experience and knowledge, the existence of funds and other intermediary vehicles that pool investments in underlying companies means that anyone can engage in this form of investing.

The rise of impact investing comes at a critical moment. Catastrophic environmental trends have created an imperative to mitigate the effects of climate change. Alarming levels of global youth unemployment—with young people three times more likely to be jobless than older people—demand heavy investment to help vulnerable individuals launch careers or become entrepreneurs. Seismic shifts in the global economy have left insufficient public funding to tackle the world's social and environmental challenges. In fact, it would be hard to overstate the extent of the tumult in which our world finds itself today.

While some of us are struggling to cope with change, others are pushing for it. A new wave of young professionals is entering the workforce, bringing with them alternative ideas about the role of business in the world. Meanwhile, this era has seen the generation and accumulation of unprecedented wealth, and the next cohort of wealthy individuals wants to approach things differently, combining their business activities with their commitments to society.

In fact, in recent years, more and more questions have been arising about the nature of capitalism itself and whether its current practice really serves our society and the planet. Many have responded with anger, as was the case at the height of the Occupy movement. Others have sought a more pragmatic approach to economic and financial transformation. At such a moment, it is hardly surprising that impact investing is attracting the interest of everyone from bankers to philanthropists to private individuals. Here is a new way of deploying capital that can combine the demand for profitability with a desire to solve social and environmental problems.

Whether it is a globally connected teenager making an online micro-loan to an African farmer or a retiring executive taking on a new role as head of a social enterprise in the United States, a new spirit of social activism is emerging. Fewer and fewer people are content to sit back and watch the world's problems unfold before them. They want to play an active role in making things different, and to do so in new ways and with the new tools and resources at their disposal. Impact investors belong to this community.

Perhaps you've already made an impact investment or are thinking of doing so. If this is the case, you are not alone. Cordes's story is just one among many of the growing community of impact investors—people and organizations seeking to use their money to solve some of the world's biggest problems. Like Cordes, they may want to help empower women to create better lives for themselves and their families. Or perhaps their goal is to help halt the destruction of precious natural resources. Whatever their aim, they want to find innovative new ways of tackling these problems.

Perhaps you have similar goals and have worked toward them by giving to nonprofits or volunteering your time. Or perhaps your values are reflected in your purchasing decisions, from Fairtrade coffee to products made from recycled packaging. Until recently, it seemed, these were the most practical ways of pursuing such goals, particularly if you weren't part of the "1 percent." Even if you made it into the *Forbes* list of the world's wealthiest, traditionally you made contributions to society by maximizing your wealth first and then thinking about addressing social and environmental challenges by giving away part of that wealth.

In addition to making grants, volunteering, or purchasing ethical products, you can now invest in enterprises or projects (such as affordable housing or sustainable forestry) that use markets to attempt to solve seemingly intractable problems or meet a social need. If these models prove successful, you may recoup your money with some profit. In some cases, these investments may perform as well as your traditional investments. In other cases, they may not (by design) meet the threshold of a traditional investment portfolio. At the same time, impact investing is not a replacement for traditional grant making, which often remains the most effective tool of philanthropy.

Impact investing offers a middle way between philanthropy and pure financial investment. It is a means of using capital to drive financial value *and* social and environmental impact simultaneously. It enables you to combine both motivations at the same time. It's a new world of opportunity.

A New Type of Business Model

For friends Shaffi Mather and Ravi Krishna, two alarming encounters with health care systems in two different parts of the world would radically alter their career paths. For Mather, it happened one evening in Kerala, India, when he found his mother choking in her sleep. He had no idea whom to call for help. His mother survived, after an intensive care unit admission, but the experience left a lasting impression. A few days later, Krishna's mother collapsed in Manhattan and was retrieved by an ambulance within four minutes.

The difference, they realized, was 911, the US telephone number that provides quick, easy access to emergency services. They also realized that if an educated Indian citizen in urban Kerala did not know what to do in an emergency, how could poor, uneducated Indians cope with one?

Mather's experience was not an isolated case. With no number to call, anyone with a medical emergency—particularly those in low-income communities—was better off calling a friend with a car or even a local rickshaw driver than an ambulance if they hoped to reach the hospital in time for life-saving care. The few ambulances in operation were often empty trucks, the same vehicles used as hearses, and there was no single phone number to call for help. As a result, people were dying needlessly.

In 2004, a group of five friends—Sweta Mangal, Naresh Jain, Manish Sacheti, Shaffi Mather, and Ravi Krishna—launched an emergency medical service in Mumbai with two ambulances. In 2005 they added 10 more ambulances. They named the service after the phone number that would connect people to it: Dial 1298 for Ambulance.

Forming a company, Ziqitza Health Care Limited, they created a business model that would use cross-subsidization to cover the cost of operations while serving poor communities. The model is simple: Those who call and ask to be taken to private hospitals pay the fee; those going to government hospitals pay little or nothing. Advertising on the sides of the vehicles generates additional revenue.

The model worked, and the company became cash flow positive in the first year of operation. By 2009, Ziqitza had experienced two years of cash positive results, demonstrating both its financial viability and its ability to address a social need.

Philanthropic contributions and start-up funds certainly helped get the business up and running. New York Presbyterian Hospital and the London Ambulance Service gave the team pro bono technical assistance and management training. In 2007, Acumen

Fund, a venture fund that uses philanthropic financing to invest in entrepreneurs with new ideas for tackling world poverty, took a $1.5 million equity stake in the enterprise to fund its expansion.

Since then, the company has attracted commercial investors such as Envision Healthcare (formerly known as EMSC), one of the world's largest ambulance providers. It has also secured government contracts, and it counts leading Indian hospitals and corporations among its clients. Because it has successfully harnessed private capital, the company has been able to expand. As of December 2013, ZHL had a turnover of $20 million, and its service now operates in the states of Kerala, Punjab, Bihar, Odisha, and Maharashtra, with plans to start operating in more states across India.

Dial 1298 for Ambulance is a great example of how a company can move along a capital curve, from concessionary investment (in this case, from Acumen Fund) and in-kind donations (the London Ambulance Service and New York–Presbyterian, a leading US health care institution) to more commercial capital (Envision Healthcare).

There was a time when the only option for financing this kind of positive social change was through philanthropy. In the case of emergency medical services, you might have funded a nonprofit organization that used its charitable donations to deliver health care services to poor communities. If the nonprofit was effective, you might have seen the return in the form of fewer needless deaths among patients with medical emergencies.

Today, however, impact investing also allows you to put your money into companies such as Dial 1298 for Ambulance, for the goal of generating a financial return while also addressing a social need. While this approach helps you as an investor meet the dual goals of social and financial impact, this way of using your money takes its impact even further. In the case of Dial 1298 for Ambulance, this means saving more lives: by 2008, the ambulance service had saved the lives of more than 4,000 Mumbai residents. ZHL now operates more than 800 ambulances, has served more than 2.4 million people, and has delivered more than 6,500 babies on board.

By making an investment rather than a donation, you pave the way for companies such as Dial 1298 for Ambulance to seek commercial capital, whether by securing loans or attracting other investors to take equity stakes. By helping these companies tap into the wider world of private investment funds, you play a role in enabling innovative solutions to be scaled up and achieve even greater impact.

Like Ron Cordes, perhaps you are a successful business leader looking to make a more meaningful impact with the wealth you have accumulated. Perhaps you are a young person inheriting your family's money or creating your own, and you reject the idea that your investment and charitable activities should work at cross purposes. Perhaps you are an institutional investor who believes that positive social and environmental impact can be combined with long-term financial performance. Or maybe you don't have much wealth to your name, or even a wealth manager at your disposal, and you want the capital you can afford to invest not just to protect you for retirement, for example, but also to help you to leave the world a better place than you found it.

Like impact investing itself, this book is not only for the superrich, or the "1 percent." While some of the investors whose stories we highlight in this book might lead you to believe otherwise, in fact, this reflects the reality that much of the pioneering work in this area has taken the form of innovative financial structures or business models that come with substantial levels of risk. As such, the risk of those investments has most appropriately been borne by the kind of investors who are able to absorb losses if their investments go bad. Increasingly, though, there are opportunities for everyone to put their money to work in this way. Impact investors are a diverse bunch, but they are united by a powerful force: a desire to meet the dual goal of achieving a financial return while generating significant social and environmental returns.

The Power of Capital Markets

Philanthropy is a powerful force for good. But the funds contributed by global philanthropy, even when combined with the development or aid budgets of many national governments (themselves facing budget constraints), add up to mere *billions*. The cost of solving problems such as water scarcity, climate change, and lack of access to health care, education, and affordable housing runs into the *trillions* of dollars.

Approached with a different mindset and strategy, these problems can often be turned into solutions that can be funded by the much larger pool of resources in the capital markets.

In virtually all sectors, you can see the effect of the gap between the demand for funds and the philanthropic resources available. Take global health. In most low-income countries, the minimum amount required to cover essential health interventions, including those needed to fight the HIV/AIDS pandemic, is estimated to be around $30 to $40 per person per year. But current spending on health in the least-developed countries is currently only about $13 per person per year.[2]

Meanwhile, in 2011 some $212 trillion existed in the world's financial stock (comprising equity market capitalization and outstanding bonds and loans),[3] and in the next 40 years, some estimate, Generation X and the Millennials could inherit up to $41 trillion from Baby Boomers.[4] Unlocking even a small percentage of this capital would expand dramatically the resources available to address the world's biggest social and environmental problems.

If we are to have any hope of solving the increasingly dynamic, complex, and messy challenges of our time, we need more investors to take this dual approach to investing. We are not suggesting that impact investing replace charitable donations, government spending, or philanthropic grants. Rather, we need more and different types of funds to complement philanthropy and strategically leverage larger and more commercial sources of funding.

As the pool of impact investors grows, their investments will make it easier for entrepreneurs with demonstrated track records to tap into a far bigger source of funding: a portion of the trillions of dollars of mainstream investment funds in global capital markets.

As investors, ranging from individuals to pension funds, seek to embed their values in the allocation of their capital, impact investing is a way of tapping into this immense financial resource. For when investors can fund talented, innovative, and committed entrepreneurs and successful local and entrepreneurial businesses, they can play a role in the creation of sustainable livelihoods, the provision of affordable public services, and the preservation of the planet. You can be part of this exciting movement. Rather than (or in addition to) writing a check to a nonprofit, you can use your funds to help create social enterprises that can become true game changers.

We live in a dynamic era of innovation, change, and new ways of thinking that could push our society in promising directions. As an investor, you can participate in this change; you have it in your power to contribute to a movement that is potentially transformative and overwhelmingly positive. This is the promise of impact investing.

So, What's Next?

In any evolving marketplace, with excitement comes confusion. If you're a newcomer to impact investing, you may have questions about what it means to become an impact investor. How is it different from venture philanthropy or socially responsible investing? What is the danger that it might cannibalize your other philanthropic resources? If you're working within an institution, could impact investing produce market-rate financial returns that are consistent with your fiduciary duty? How can you be sure your impact investments will yield financial returns but also deliver the kind of impact that will contribute to human development and help secure our natural resources?

If you're a more seasoned impact investor, you might be wrestling with additional questions. What types of liquidity opportunities can these investments provide? Is impact investing an asset class or something that crosses different asset classes? How will you be held accountable for meeting your social and environmental objectives? Who will you hold accountable for meeting your social and environmental objectives? Are there enough investment-ready deals out there?

To answer these questions and help move impact investing into the mainstream, we offer practical advice and real-world stories showing how impact investing can bring about tangible change. It's time to pull back the curtain on impact investing and showcase the role it can play in solving some of our biggest global challenges by tapping into large pools of capital funds. For, without engaging a broad community of investors, this promising means of mobilizing private capital will fail to meet its full potential.

The Power of Impact Investing reflects what we, as its authors, have witnessed in recent years. We have been both close observers and supporters of this evolving investment approach. Since taking over as president of the Rockefeller Foundation, Judith has been refocusing its activities to meet today's complex challenges, shaping innovations that create resilience to twenty-first-century risks and ensure more inclusive economies. Margot, who joined the Rockefeller Foundation in 2006, has worked on building the infrastructure necessary to advance the field of impact investing and on initiatives promoting economic development and quality jobs for low-wage workers. She is now working on two start-up impact enterprises as a fellow at the Nathan Cummings Foundation.

We have been in the rooms where critical impact investment discussions have taken place—and on the ground, where we see impact dollars creating real social benefit. We have seen the problems out there and witnessed the emergence of innovative ideas to address them. In our work, we connect the theoretical framework of impact investing with its real-world implications for communities, our environment, and other stakeholders. Our roles in philanthropy, and our engagements with the private sector as members of multiple boards of directors of global companies, mean we can speak candidly and objectively about the opportunities and the risks. But as part of the organization that was among the architects of impact investing, we are certainly not impartial observers. The Rockefeller Foundation has so far invested more than $40 million in building the field and over $100 million in impact investments from its endowment. We believe in the power of impact investing. We believe it offers a middle way—an opportunity to complement precious philanthropic capital and to promote market-driven solutions.

With this in mind, we write this book with two goals. First, by providing basic guidelines for how to engage, we wish to help those of you on the sidelines determine whether impact investing is the right approach when it comes to meeting some of your investment and social objectives.

Second, we aim to speak frankly about what remains to be done to ensure that impact investing continues to be a viable means of investing, not just in the United States and Europe, but also in regions where new wealth can be harnessed. While Asia, Africa, and Latin America have been *destinations* for impact investing capital for several years, emerging market investors remain comparatively untapped *sources* of capital. And this capital will only grow as patterns of global wealth shift and high-net-worth individuals are located in Beijing and São Paulo as well as in New York and London. Increasingly, wherever you are in the world, as an impact investor you are not alone.

We do not mean to imply that impact investing is the right option for every investor, particularly because large volumes of evidence confirming its positive long-term returns have yet to emerge. Nor are we suggesting that impact investing can provide solutions to all our problems or replace public funding or philanthropy. In most countries, governments remain the largest source of financing for service delivery and the provision of public goods. Foundations play a vital role, providing the first layer of risk capital, convening stakeholders, and finding innovations that can be applied to social problems.

These sources of finance are essential for reaching the poorest communities who cannot be served by markets and for supporting democracy, civil rights, the arts, and other public goods that do not lend themselves to market-based models. And philanthropic funds are needed to help build the infrastructure that will underpin the growth of impact investing markets.

The truth is if we are to make a real impact on the world's biggest problems, we need to use every tool at our disposal. We believe that impact investing offers an additional tool, one with tremendous potential. Take the rapid growth of unplanned urban communities in much of the developing world, which presents serious challenges to the sustainability of natural resources and to the health and quality of life of millions of people. The sanitation and potable water concerns associated with slum expansion are immense—but so is the opportunity to invest in everything from affordable housing to innovative systems for water provision to urban micro-schools that will enable the next generation to break out of the cycle of poverty. In solving these and other challenges, we believe impact investing can be a powerful instrument of change. And we want to help you and many others make use of it.

In writing this book, we want to help make more funds available to address big global challenges. We want to help create a world where an impact investment choice will be as easy to make as a philanthropic donation; where a sophisticated ecosystem of advisers and measurement tools will give even the most cautious the confidence to dip their toes in these waters; where considering the social and environmental impact of a financial investment is simply part of the natural order of things.

But most of all, we want you to share our excitement about the opportunities that are opening up for investors. We want you not only to grasp the "how" of impact investing but also to gain an understanding of the "why." At the Rockefeller Foundation, we believe that impact investing has the potential to transform how we view problem solving from something deemed the sole responsibility of government or development aid to an opportunity for diverse actors to unlock new sources of capital and introduce novel approaches to human development and environmental conservation. Meanwhile, for some of the investors we'll hear from in the following chapters, the "why" is simpler: they want to have their values and goals reflected in as many of their investment activities as possible.

Whatever your reason for reading this book, we hope it will help you explore impact investing in depth, from the external forces that shape it to where the industry is headed and its performance so far. Before we begin, a quick note on the scope of this endeavor. As authors, our intention is to be illustrative, rather than comprehensive, with a focus on early activities and future directions of the impact investing field. Therefore, we could not include all of the concepts or leaders who helped create this dynamic universe, and we encourage those readers who wish to delve deeper to explore the resources and further readings in the appendix.

Now, on to what you will find in the pages to come. In chapters 1 and 2, we'll take a detailed look at what it means to be an impact investor, the different objectives that can be pursued, the asset classes and investment vehicles emerging, and how a range of investors, from individuals to institutions, can participate.

In chapter 3, "Impact Investment Opportunities," we'll look at the range of investment opportunities—that is, the innovative enterprises that are the recipients of impact investment funds. In chapter 4, "Support Systems," we'll assess the infrastructure needed to support impact investing, from measurement systems to policy choices. Chapter 5, "A Global Movement," shows you how impact investing is developing around the world.

Finally, and most important, in chapter 6, "Getting Started," we will show how you, the investor, can harness the powerful idea of using for-profit funds to help change the world. In the appendix, you will find an even fuller listing of available resources.

Let's get started.

CHAPTER 1

What Is Impact Investing?

The pieces of jewelry created for Liberty United, a company founded by entrepreneur Peter Thum, are striking, highly unusual objects. With simple, chunky contemporary designs, they draw attention to those who wear them. And they don't come cheap—rings start at $85 and necklaces run between $95 and $1,485. But beyond design and price tag, the most noticeable feature is the stamp of a serial number prominently displayed on each piece. The numbers do not signify the relative purity of the metal used or the sequence in which the pieces were produced. Rather, it's the serial number of the gun from which the piece was made.

Thum is the founder of Ethos Water, a venture that helped half a million people across the world gain access to clean water and sanitation. He created Liberty United in 2012 to tackle the problem of gun violence in the United States. He has some experience in this. With a similar goal, he created Fonderie 47 in 2009 to help eradicate some of the weapons and small arms responsible for so many deaths and injuries in Africa. Every piece is made from part of an AK-47 and bears that weapon's serial number; the money raised by the sale of the jewelry is used to help fund the removal and destruction of more firearms.

The company puts a number on how many weapons the purchase of each piece destroys. For example, a set of cufflinks in 14-karat white gold and blackened steel costing $11,000 destroys 30 assault rifles in Africa. Not only do the cufflinks bear the serial number of the gun from which they were made, but the buyer of those cufflinks also receives the serial numbers of the 30 weapons the purchase helped destroy. "The question was how to transform the problem itself and put it in the hands of someone in a form that makes it connected but completely different," says Thum.

Through Liberty United, Thum plans to do the same in the United States by enlisting artists and artisans to turn bullets and gunmetal into high-end jewelry, using proceeds from the jewelry sales to contribute to tackling gun violence and entering partnerships with city authorities working to reclaim illegally possessed firearms. The impact of such alliances goes further. Through a partnership with the City of Philadelphia, for example, the Philadelphia Anti-Drug/ Anti-Violence Network will be able to increase the safety in city communities through its collaboration with the Youth Violence Reduction Partnership, which helps people access resources such as drug treatment, health care services, and employment training and mentoring.[5]

Like many, Thum believes that for-profit businesses with a mission can achieve the scale needed to tackle big, global social problems. And for someone wanting to use their impact investment funds to tackle gun violence, Liberty United might be a good choice—it's a company that both helps take guns off the street and raises awareness of the issue of gun violence through the production and marketing of eye-catching jewelry with designs that are guaranteed to spark a conversation. Meanwhile, the success of Liberty United as a high-end retail business would make it a promising investment from a financial standpoint, thus meeting the dual purpose that is at the heart of all impact investments.

The intentional pursuit of social or environmental benefit alongside profit is what makes Liberty United an impact investment. This approach is related to, but different from, other approaches to using the capital markets to bring about social change. In this chapter, we'll show you both how impact investing sits within the broad spectrum of social investments and how it represents a different way forward. We'll also discuss the variations within impact investing itself, from the different objectives of investors to the investment vehicles available to them. First, let's look at the landscape from which impact investing emerged.

A Model with Deep Roots

The idea of harnessing the power of the market in alignment with investor values dates back to the 19th century, when religious institutions sought to avoid investing in "sin" stocks, such as the tobacco or alcohol industries. In the 1970s the socially responsible investment (SRI) industry started expanding. As we'll explain in more depth, SRI investors are motivated by many of the same concerns as impact investors, and SRI investments have often served as a bridge between traditional investing and impact investing.

Perhaps the oldest form of impact investing itself is microfinance. For more than 30 years, the practice of making small loans to the world's poorest people has proved a powerful tool in the battle to eradicate poverty. With its beginnings in Bangladesh and Latin America in the 1970s and '80s, microfinance rose to global prominence in 2006 with the award of the Nobel Prize to Muhammad Yunus, the Bangladeshi banker who turned his early experiments with small loans to groups of villagers into a vast self-supporting network of millions of borrowers (mostly women).

Meanwhile, in the United States, the Community Reinvestment Act in 1977 created a network of community development financial institutions (CDFIs) to provide mortgages and other financial services to communities underserved by mainstream banks. Many CDFIs work with local organizations to create employment opportunities and provide affordable housing and financial literacy training. Some of them have also helped to create innovative investment opportunities that promote additional benefits, such as environmental sustainability and improving access to healthy food.

Alongside these seeds of the impact investing industry, the philanthropic sector has been looking to business for ways of making a greater impact. Part of this has meant embracing some of the outcome-oriented principles and practices of the business sector, as in the case of venture philanthropy, which we will describe in the next section.

Meanwhile, from the 1990s the concept of corporate social responsibility gained momentum, with companies working to manage the complex effects of their business activities on society and the environment. In a 2011 *Harvard Business Review* paper,[6] Michael Porter and Mark Kramer's concept of "shared value" made explicit the growing recognition that companies can produce better results not just for shareholders, but also for employees, customers, suppliers, and the communities they operate in.

These and other activities ignited the imaginations of investors, entrepreneurs, and philanthropists who were rejecting the old notion of maximizing profit with one hand and giving away charity with the other. The notion that businesses and investors could do both began to take shape, as did the idea that when social or environmental missions are combined with business models, the potential impact increases while simultaneously generating profits (which can be plowed back into the social mission). It was the emergence of a world where new perspectives, experimentation, and innovation could thrive—where mobile phones could bring access to financial services to the unbanked, where pay-as-you go models could make solar power affordable and accessible in the poorest rural communities. This blending of business ideas with theories of social change opened the doors to the possibility of accelerating human development and more effectively conserving natural resources, all at a greater scale than government or philanthropy alone could provide.

In 2007 the Rockefeller Foundation convened a group of investors, entrepreneurs, and philanthropists at its Bellagio Conference Center in Italy. Participants were asked what would enable them and others to put more capital to work for social and environmental benefit. By the end of the meeting, the term *impact investing* had been coined.[7] At a second meeting, in 2008, a blueprint was in place for building the field. But while impact investing has emerged from a world where values and business models have been converging, it offers something new and different.

What Impact Investing Is *Not*

Impact investors are members of a diverse community of individuals and organizations, all of which want to tap into the power of business models to provide new solutions to social and environmental problems. So how exactly does impact investing differ from other investments and models that seek to make a positive impact on people and the planet? Generally speaking, impact investing sits on a continuum, with SRI investing on one side and venture philanthropy on the other. The distinctions can get blurry, but impact investing differs from its neighboring fields in important ways. In this section, we will define and show how other models relate to or are different from impact investing.

Socially Responsible Investing

Socially responsible investing is a form of capital deployment in which a financial return is expected but that incorporates social or environmental values into investment decisions. With more than $3.74 trillion under management in the United States alone,[8] the SRI movement is large as well as diverse.

SRI investors and fund managers have traditionally excluded companies or sectors that "do harm," but more recently, SRI has expanded to embrace positive performance by integrating environmental, social, or governance (ESG) factors into the long-term financial analysis of a company. This approach to SRI—modeled by funds such as David Blood and Al Gore's Generation Investment Management—often emphasizes the cost savings or risk mitigation of good long-term environmental and social practices. Generation Investment Management and some of its peers have begun to describe this approach to investing as "sustainable capitalism."[9]

Still another investment practice that is generally categorized as SRI is to hold stock in publicly traded companies and use that power to bring shareholder resolutions, or proposals, to companies to induce companies, say, to do more to reduce their carbon emissions or bring an end to unethical practices. This approach is gaining momentum as activist shareholders use increasingly sophisticated approaches to influence corporate behavior. During the 2013 proxy season (when many companies hold their annual shareholder meetings), 110 shareholder resolutions were filed with 94 US companies on issues such as climate change, supply chain sustainability, and water-related risks.[10]

Impact investing is related to those investment approaches, but is also distinct from them. Perhaps the best way to convey this distinction is to build on the example of Liberty United, which we discussed at the beginning of this chapter. An SRI investor with a mission to reduce gun violence might create a portfolio of investments that excludes "bad" companies such as arms dealers and gun makers, or might use his or her power as a shareholder to influence those companies' business strategies. By contrast, impact investors might put money in Liberty United (or a similar business) in order to make a positive investment in a company that is proactively working to address the problem of gun violence.

Venture Philanthropy

On the other side of impact investing sits venture philanthropy. Venture philanthropy has been around for decades. One of the first uses of the term occurred in 1969, when during hearings before the Committee on Ways and Means on foundation tax reform, John D. Rockefeller III (grandson of the founder of the Rockefeller Foundation) described venture philanthropy as "the imaginative pursuit of less conventional charitable purposes than those normally undertaken by established public charitable organizations."[11] In the 1990s—especially after the publication in 1997 of an influential *Harvard Business Review* article, "Virtuous Capital: What Foundations Can Learn from Venture Capitalists"[12]—this type of philanthropy gained momentum.

Rather like venture capitalists, venture philanthropists put their funds into start-ups or rapidly growing organizations. Importantly, venture philanthropists supply not only grant funds but also assistance on things such as building a business plan, creating a management structure, enhancing operational efficiency, and measuring and reporting progress. Venture philanthropists aim to increase the impact of their funding by supporting innovation, risking failure, and ultimately helping to identify and scale up approaches to social and environmental change that are effective, efficient, and sustainable. And unlike other funders, venture philanthropists put in place an exit strategy. In other words, they hope their investments will be so successful that eventually their funding will no longer be needed. However, while venture philanthropy uses many of the terms, principles, and practices of for-profit investing, it remains a *grant-making* model—unlike impact investing, venture philanthropy funds are provided without the requirement of an expected financial return.

So, How Is Impact Investing Different?

While impact investing shares some ground with these forms of capital deployment, it represents a powerful additional tool in the battle to improve lives and solve some of the world's biggest problems. Although the distinctions between impact investing and other types of social investments are not always clear cut, many of the characteristics shared by impact investors differentiate them from other types of socially responsible investors.

So what are these distinguishing characteristics? Here are some of the most important:

- At the heart of impact investing is the presence of dual objectives—the desire actively to achieve positive social or environmental results as well as financial ones.

- Impact investing may complement philanthropy and be used by philanthropists, but it is not philanthropy—unlike grants, impact investments are made with an expectation of financial return.
- Impact investing is more than "doing no harm"—it is a positive investment made in an enterprise that has the potential to solve a specific problem or deliver a particular service while also turning a profit or at least becoming financially self-sustaining.
- Both impact investors and the businesses in which they invest— we call them impact enterprises, although they are often referred to as social enterprises—track relevant financial as well as social and environmental performance metrics across their portfolios or enterprises.

Yet, while united by these characteristics, impact investing is also diverse. It includes microfinance, community development finance, conservation and renewable energy finance, and the growing number of opportunities in education, health, nutrition, and other aspects of human development and environmental protection. It differs by asset class, return expectation, sector, and geography. Impact investments can take the form of equity, debt, cash deposits, or another hybrid form. In short, impact investing provides a universe of opportunities that, like mainstream investments, allow for individual choices to be made on everything from risk appetite and time horizon to sector and geographic location.

Now we'll look at how different objectives—environmental versus social, or broad based versus highly targeted—guide impact investing decisions.

The Objectives

As a Peace Corps volunteer in West Africa in 2004, Sam Goldman learned that vast numbers of people living in the developing world relied on kerosene lamps as their only source of light at night. He knew that these emitted a good deal of carbon dioxide, were expensive to buy and maintain, and weren't productive sources of light. "I lived with kerosene lamps for four years; that's how I learned," he explains. But it was the burns a neighbor's son sustained from a kerosene-powered fridge that drew Goldman's attention to the dangers of this form of energy. "Kerosene burns from lanterns were frequent, and I learned how frequent they were through more research," he says. This prompted him to enroll in a class at the Institute of Design at Stanford focusing on creating transformative, affordable products for the world's poorest people. What he and a fellow student, Ned Tozun, produced was a low-cost solar lantern that was to change lives for millions.

As of December 2013, their company, d.light, had provided more than 7 million school-age children with solar lighting, saved families $870 million in energy-related expenses, and offset more than 2 million tons of carbon emissions.[13] As a private company, d.light has chosen not to disclose information on its sales or profitability. It's hard to underestimate the impact of making this technology available to poor communities. By replacing dirty kerosene with solar power, d.light helps families avoid the illness and deaths that can be caused by inhaling the fumes from kerosene lamps. Solar power provides a more affordable source of power for poor communities that previously relied on kerosene lamps, because they are no longer sinking costs into kerosene (and candles and disposable batteries) month after month. And any extra money is usually spent on health and education—and on more energy. Perhaps most critically, the availability of a cheap, clean source of lighting means that children can study at night, improving their performance at school, and microbusinesses can operate for longer hours, increasing the income they generate.

Investors in d.light include self-identified impact investors Omidyar Network and Acumen Fund, and more mainstream investors such as Nexus Venture Partners, a leading Indian venture capital firm; DJF, a venture capital firm with a global presence through a network of partner funds; and Garage Technology Ventures, a seed-stage and early-stage venture capital fund based in Silicon Valley. The company decided on a mix of mission-driven and commercial investors as a way to manage its financial and social objectives.

In providing lamps, one could say that d.light makes a direct impact by addressing energy poverty. The benefits of d.light's services, however, are myriad: changing lives, reducing carbon emissions, improving education, and increasing livelihood opportunities for poor families. Investors in d.light may therefore hope to achieve one or more of a range of impact objectives.

Other investors might choose to be more targeted in their investments, directing funding to specific social or environmental issues in certain countries or regions. The Lyme Timber Company, for example, focuses on the acquisition and sustainable management of timberlands, providing impact investors with the opportunity to finance forest conservation in the United States. Lyme Timber also highlights the fact that the destinations for impact capital need not be enterprises—they can be "real assets" such as forests, housing developments, and schools.

Often investors wishing to have a highly targeted impact will invest directly in companies. The Kellogg Foundation, for example, has allocated $100 million of its endowment assets for impact investments into companies that advance its mission to improve the lives of vulnerable children.[14] This focus has led the foundation to invest directly in companies such as Wireless Generation, which creates innovative tools, systems, and services that help educators customize curricula and improve assessment. However, the proliferation of specialized funds and intermediaries means that investors can increasingly have a targeted impact without investing directly in companies. Kellogg has also, for example, invested in NCB Capital Impact (a US nonprofit and certified community development financial institution) to administer loans to healthy food providers in its target locations of New Mexico, Mississippi, New Orleans (Louisiana), and Michigan.[15]

As an impact investor, you may want to use your funds to advance environmental goals. Or you may prefer to focus on human development, through investments in companies or funds that address issues such as health care or food security. You may want to target your investment narrowly and become personally involved in the companies you fund. Or you may want your investments to "do good" in whatever ways are possible without causing major disruption to your existing asset allocation or financial management strategies.

Impact investing allows for all these options. The beauty of this approach to investing is that it can accommodate a wide variety of goals, both social and financial.

A Diversity of Goals

Although all impact investments, by definition, actively seek the dual goals of financial and social returns, the relative primacy of these objectives may vary considerably from one investment to the next. As an impact investor, depending on the importance you place on the different returns, you might describe yourself as a *finance-first* or *impact-first* investor.

These terms emerged shortly after the term *impact investing* was coined, in order to distinguish between investors whose primary intent was to create impact (impact-first investors) from those who had an obligation to make impact investments that maximized financial returns (finance-first investors). While it is overly simplistic to place impact investors in one of two buckets, and the terms have since been criticized for unnecessarily polarizing investors, it is nonetheless necessary to distinguish between investors who require competitive financial returns and those who can accept a concessionary, or below-market, risk-adjusted rate of financial return in exchange for pursuing high or specifically targeted social or environmental impacts.

For example, TIAA-CREF, one of the largest fund managers in the United States, requires impact investments to earn a market rate of financial return. It manages $14 billion in assets across a suite of "Social Choice" products, which includes a $600 million portfolio of social investments in relatively mature sectors such as inclusive finance, affordable housing, and community and economic development. For its part, in its program-related investments, the MacArthur Foundation prioritizes social impact and targets investments that do not have an ordinary risk-return profile—whether because they seek a concessionary rate of return or take a position (in terms of length, illiquidity, and so on) that commercial investors would not take. Individuals and families can fall into either or both categories—we know people whose impact investments are intended to "outperform Wall Street," and others who are willing to take levels of risk in pursuit of their impact goals with the understanding they may not see any returns, and may even lose money.

In practice, this distinction can become fuzzy, and it is further complicated by the fact that different investors assess risk differently and may not agree on what a "risk-adjusted market rate" of return should be for a given investment. Because social enterprises often have business models that are innovative and unconventional, and the markets in which they operate are new or poorly understood, they are often ill suited to traditional risk-analysis approaches. For example, microfinance, which lends money to poor people without credit history or formal collateral, would be considered extremely risky by some analysts, while others might examine repayment history and determine it to be a relatively safe investment.

So, surprising though it may seem, it's possible to find impact-first and finance-first investors investing in the same deals. As the industry evolves, new due diligence and measurement metrics will be needed to take account of the complexity of returns—from financial to social and environmental—that are possible in impact investing. (We will look at some of these measurement systems in chapter 4, "Support Systems.")

Another complicating factor is the interplay between social impact and financial returns. Many investors assume social impact must be traded off against greater profit, or vice versa, because of the higher costs of serving poorer clients, paying higher wages, or engaging in environmental remediation. Others argue that if a company's core business model is inherently impactful (if, for example, it produces solar lanterns for poor people), its profitability and social impact should grow together. Still others say that while pursuing social impact and profit may involve short-term tradeoffs, these goals converge in the long term.

As an investor, your worldview and specific objectives will likely influence where you come out on these questions. In our view, the relationship between financial and social returns (that is, whether they are positively correlated or at odds) depends on the particular investment and the type of impact being sought.

Investment Vehicles

Impact investments run the gamut of traditional asset classes, from private debt, bilateral loan agreements, deposits, and guarantees to equity-like debt, private equity, and real assets such as real estate, gold, or oil. Investment terms and structures may replicate those found in the mainstream investment world, or they may be new and bespoke arrangements that have been created to serve a unique function. There are, for example, a number of impact investing funds that use a standard "2 and 20" private equity fund structure, which takes capital from limited partners and places it with companies (e.g., those that provide health services to the world's poorest communities). Fund managers are often compensated through a 2 percent management fee and 20 percent of the eventual profits of the fund.

In other cases, standard investment structures may be tweaked to serve their dual objectives, as is the case with Core Innovation Capital, which, seeing access to financial services as a powerful tool for improving life for low- and moderate-income Americans, invests in innovative companies that provide financial services to underbanked consumers in the United States. This approach uses a combination of financial and social targets to determine how profits are distributed among the fund manager and limited partners.

In addition, entirely new arrangements have been created to serve a function that traditional investment vehicles cannot. Social impact bonds, for example (which we will describe in chapter 3, "Impact Investment Opportunities") are distinct from traditional bonds, in spite of their name.

As an investor, you can therefore construct a portfolio of impact investments that resemble your existing traditional investments, or one that has been entirely tailored to your particular social or environmental objectives—or you may do a combination of both. Yet, even among the forms of impact investing familiar in the mainstream investment world, the intent of investors to create social impact is what sets these instruments apart from mainstream capital investments. This distinction is perhaps the most crucial among finance-first impact investments designed to generate market rates of financial return.

Conclusion

Back in 2007 and 2008, when the Rockefeller Foundation convened its impact investment meetings at the Bellagio Center, impact investing as an industry was in its infancy. Since then, it has taken off far more quickly than even the enthusiasts at Bellagio could have imagined. Tremendous growth has been seen in the number of organizations in the field, the networks that have emerged to support them, the amount of capital being mobilized, the variety of financial products on offer, and the research available to those who want to learn more. The infrastructure needed to make this approach viable has been expanding, too, with the advent of new measurement tools and reporting standards.

Meanwhile, the emergence of a new generation of enterprises makes this form of investing possible. Whether a farmers' cooperative in Ghana, an affordable housing complex in Baltimore, a string of maternity clinics in Bangladesh, an off-grid solar business in rural Tanzania, or a Fairtrade food retailer in California, these enterprises are applying market-based approaches to the urgent problems around them. While once their leaders might have set up a nonprofit and applied for grant funding, today they are tackling these problems through business models that not only provide financial sustainability but whose solutions have the potential to be replicated and scaled up to achieve far greater impact. (These businesses, "impact enterprises," are the recipients of impact investors' funds; we'll take a look at what these people and organizations do in chapter 2, "Who Are the Impact Investors?")

The impact investment community has been expanding rapidly, too. Once confined to a small group of committed pioneers, investors now range from private bankers to institutional investors to the board members of nonprofits. And many are optimistic that the size and diversity of the industry can only continue to grow. This is certainly the belief of Luther Ragin, president and CEO of the Global Impact Investing Network (GIIN), the leading nonprofit organization working to develop a successful impact investing industry. "Given the breadth of the impact investing market," he says, "there are significant and varied opportunities for investors working across asset classes and with a wide range of risk/return expectations to address some of the world's most pressing problems through their investment activities."

Some individuals and organizations have already embarked on impact investing. Others are just starting out. Eager to learn more and start their impact investing journey, they want to find new ways to put their money to work for the things they care about. You may be among them. In the next chapter, we'll look at the wide range of individuals and organizations engaging in impact investing and the different approaches they are taking to achieve their dual impact goals.

CHAPTER 2

Who Are the Impact Investors?

Having worked for several years in Central and Eastern Europe and seen firsthand the environmental degradation taking place there, Helene Marsh, a San Francisco–based environmental consultant, became passionate about combating climate change. She went back to school, graduated with a master's degree in environmental science and management, and constructed her family's home to meet the Leadership in Energy & Environmental Design (LEED) platinum certification. But she wanted her values reflected in all aspects of her life—and that included her investments. "I feel like there are a lot of things I can't change in the world," she says. "But I can change my personal choices."

She had no investment expertise; nor did she have enough assets to establish a family foundation or to lock her funds up in long-term, illiquid investments. But she wanted to do what she could. Her money had been managed by conventional investment management firms for 15 years. She started by questioning her existing managers about the environmental aspects of her investments, but found their answers unsatisfactory. Then, when doing a Google search for a "sustainable investment advisory," she came across Veris Wealth Partners, a boutique advisory firm that helps clients align their money with their missions. Upon cold-calling the firm, she was impressed with its approach and initially placed $1 million there, invested largely with best-in-class SRI managers who screened out environmentally harmful companies. She was pleased with their performance.

In the meantime, Marsh educated herself on the topic of socially responsible investment and impact investing. The following year, she decided to transfer the balance of her investable assets to Veris. Having purged her investments of environmentally damaging companies through SRI, she is now beginning to invest in opportunities that intentionally generate a positive impact on the health of the planet.

Marsh is just one type of impact investor. Another is J.B. Pritzker, the venture capitalist, entrepreneur, and philanthropist, and someone who is passionate about early childhood education. Like many, he recognizes the impact on society of equipping its youngest members with the tools they need to go on to higher education, to enter the workforce, and ultimately to create a successful career and a prosperous life. Early learning, Pritzker says, "reduces social and economic inequality and builds a better workforce and a stronger nation."[16] As president of the J.B. and M.K. Pritzker Family Foundation, he provided grants to support research and programs targeting children in the world's poorest communities. He was looking for a "version 2.0" that would build on this work by experimenting with a creative approach to using private investment capital to leverage the capital markets and government spending for greater positive impacts.

At the Clinton Global Initiative America conference in June 2013, Pritzker announced the launch of a multimillion-dollar investment initiative designed to make more high-quality early education programs available to disadvantaged children across the United States. He worked with Imprint Capital, a dedicated impact investment adviser, to build and manage this new program, which made its first investment in a "pay for success" transaction in which Pritzker took a subordinate position to catalyze Goldman Sachs in providing a combined $7 million toward high-quality, center-based early childhood education.

Pritzker's $2.4 million is instrumental in allowing 3,500 high-needs children to come off waitlists and into high-performing preschools across Salt Lake City and Park City, Utah. Returns to the investors will be based on the cost savings made as more children remain on track as they progress through their schooling in what is known as social impact bond (SIB) or a pay-for-success deal. (We will discuss SIBs in detail in chapter 3, "Impact Investment Opportunities.")

Marsh and Pritzker differ in a number of important ways. Marsh is seeking a rate of financial return that will keep her family comfortable—she is willing to sacrifice the "greed factor" that she believes comes with fossil fuel investments, but she cannot afford to risk significant amounts of money in unproven and illiquid investment structures. Pritzker is willing to take significant risk to attract leveraged investors and drive long-term policy change—a difference that is not surprising given their relative wealth and the percentage of their assets being deployed to impact investments. Pritzker is passionate about social issues, specifically education, whereas Marsh is generally passionate about the environment. Pritzker wanted to roll up his proverbial sleeves and put together an original, multifaceted investment structure, whereas Marsh wanted to invest passively in products that resemble her existing investments as closely as possible. Marsh believes that "the amount of good you can do is about personal circumstances—the level of risk you can take, the amount of liquidity you need. And if you come from a traditional bread-and-butter approach to wealth management, it takes a while to get ramped up."

Alongside Marsh and Pritzker is a range of impact investors, from institutional investors and banks to family offices and individual investors. And they vary in the size of their funds and their appetite for risk. Institutional investors such as pension funds are where the lion's share of global capital is located, and they often have the in-house expertise and capacity needed to identify, perform due diligence on, and manage a range of investments. However, they are legally constrained by fiduciary regulations, which generally prevent them from doing things that could reduce the financial return they generate. They are thus confined to investments whose returns can be considered market rate, which limits the type of investments they can make. By contrast, family offices and individuals have greater latitude to engage in a broad range of impact investing forms and have often been at the forefront of innovation in the field.

As an impact investor, you are part of a diverse and dynamic community made up of individuals and organizations with varying degrees of financial resources and experience, a diversity of goals and objectives and differences in their approaches to investing. In this chapter, we will show you some examples of the different types of members of the expanding community of impact investors.

Individuals and Family Offices

Elaine Nonneman was raised in Cleveland, Ohio, where her family ran (and still operates) an auto parts manufacturing business. She left Cleveland when she went to college, but during her visits back, she found the city suffering. Jobs were shed as companies moved out or were shut down. "It saddened me that every time I'd go back, I'd see more closures and signs of blighted areas," she says. Nonneman was an active philanthropist, but felt that a lot of charitable approaches were ill suited to alleviating poverty.

When funding a scholarship program through the Cleveland Foundation, she came across a description of Evergreen Cooperatives in one of its newsletters. The Evergreen Cooperatives are a set of worker-owned green cooperative companies seeded by the Cleveland Foundation and other donors. The latest to be set up was the Green City Growers, a large hydroponic greenhouse designed to be the region's largest provider of lettuce.

Elaine was interested in cooperative economic models and passionate about local food systems and organic agriculture, so unsurprisingly, she was immediately attracted to the Green City Growers. More surprising was how she set about supporting it. "I had a lot of bond investments, where yields were very low," she explains. "I thought the greenhouse could provide a way to generate income that wasn't too taxing on the business. I saw it as an alternative to my existing investments."

She made a $150,000 loan over five years at 2.5 percent interest. "Initially, I thought about charging a higher rate, but I decided the terms should be friendlier. Also, this rate was competitive with the yield on my other fixed income investments at the time."

Elaine made several trips to Cleveland to visit the greenhouse and meet with key management and partners as part of her due diligence. She continues to monitor its progress during visits to her hometown and has been pleased with its progress since it opened in February 2013. However, she decided to modify the terms of the loan so it would be interest-only for the first year. "The greenhouse is doing well, but it isn't yet break-even. As a private individual, I can be more flexible than the government," she says. "So I can modify the terms if it seems like it is in the interests of both parties."

Of course, you don't have to be an accredited investor like Marsh, Pritzker, or Nonneman to make impact investments. While historically most individual investors have been "high-net-worth individuals," meaning they have (individually or with their spouses) at least $1 million in investable assets, an increasing number of opportunities are available to all individuals.

For example, more than 3,000 people have invested over $5 million in community solar projects throughout the United States through a platform called Mosaic. With as little as $25, people can finance solar projects that save money for schools, homeowners, or other community-based institutions while reducing carbon emissions through clean energy generation. One such solar installation was at the McGuire-Dix-Lakehurst military base in Fort Dix, New Jersey, the nation's first tri-service military base, which reduced energy bills for base residents while helping the US Department of Defense meet its voluntary goal of 25 percent renewable energy by 2025. In another case, a solar system powers the Pinnacle Charter School, one of the largest public charter schools in Colorado, with more than 2,000 students. The solar project could save the school up to $1.6 million in electricity costs over the project's lifetime while enabling thousands of K–12 students to learn about clean energy.

In chapter 6 we'll describe more of the opportunities available to retail investors and discuss the changes in crowdfunding regulation that are paving the way for more people and organizations to become far more active as impact investors.

For individual investors, the reasons for making impact investments vary widely. For many, the opportunity to make a difference locally—in the places where they live, work, have accumulated their wealth, or are already active as philanthropists—is a strong motivating force. If supporting your local community is high on your agenda, you may proactively identify and craft local investment opportunities as Nonneman did. Increasingly, though, you may be able to identify an existing organization that already does this. For example, Coastal Enterprises Inc. offers a debt product that raises "patient capital" from accredited Maine individuals and family foundations to provide loans to small businesses, affordable housing organizations, community facilities, and natural resource enterprises.

For other individuals, impact investing is a logical extension of goals they have pursued in other aspects of their lives. Kim Jordan, cofounder of Colorado-based New Belgium Brewing Company, describes herself as a relative newcomer to impact investing. She spent decades building New Belgium as a values-driven business, innovating in methods that would minimize its environmental footprint and build employee wealth. She elected to make the company a B Corporation (which we will describe in chapter 4), and in 2013 she structured an exit for herself, her sons, and the company's six other managers by selling 100 percent of the company to its employees. Jordan recalls that "there we were, myself and my boys, with all of this money. One of the board members, who is a particular friend of mine, said, 'Let's talk about what it is you want to do with it,' and I realized I wanted to do what we had done at New Belgium: create environmental benefit, pioneer innovation, and make an overall commitment to moving the field forward." Jordan and her sons each used 50 percent of their new wealth to start a foundation and invested its assets and the balance of their personal wealth with specialist wealth manager Sonen Capital. Her investment strategy reflects the ethos and the specific goals of New Belgium. "It seems odd to me to come from a values-driven business but say, 'In our investments, the sky is the limit—go for big oil!'" Jordan says. "You work hard to make choices that live with a certain set of values, and not to carry that over to your investments doesn't make any sense to me."

Some investors are drawn to impact investing by the idea of helping to get an innovative start-up off the ground in a developing country. With enterprises scattered across the globe and often tiny in scale, doing this alone is extremely difficult for an individual investor or family office. Navigating the relevant legal issues and identifying terms that meet the needs of both investors and entrepreneurs can be particularly challenging. In this case, you might turn to a network or wealth adviser for help. Or you may actively seek to raise additional capital in order to defray administrative costs. San Francisco–based Charly Kleissner, for example, decided to invest in Healthpoint Services—a company that provides health services to the world's poorest communities in rural and semi-urban parts of India—after he met its founder through a social enterprise incubator program at Santa Clara University. Rather than do the deal alone, Kleissner put together a small syndicate of like-minded investors, each of whom was willing to invest on similar terms.

Still others are drawn to impact investing by its emphasis on innovation. Ion Yadigaroglu, managing principal at the Palo Alto–based Capricorn Investment Group (which manages the assets of eBay founder Jeff Skoll and others), is clear that his firm's aspiration is to outperform Wall Street on financial terms. However, he believes that in California (in contrast to the way wealth is amassed in many parts of the world) there is a "unique belief that wealth creation is tied to innovation," and he explains that his approach to making impact investments—which range from solar power and electric vehicles to cost-effective health care delivery—stems from his principals' desire to "extend that California magic to as much of the economy as possible."

Capricorn takes a highly active role in managing its $5 billion in assets, just as Nonneman and Pritzker were active in designing the investments just described. Individual investors and family offices have unique flexibility in setting their own multifaceted investment strategies and targets. But not everyone is able to spend the time needed to identify, structure, and manage direct or complex investments. Some may therefore invest through specialized funds or other intermediaries (as we will explain in the following chapter) or use the assistance of a wealth adviser (or both). And there is evidence that more of us would like to do this. In a poll of more than 4,000 US–based individuals from households that earn more than $80,000 a year, 48 percent said they were interested in impact investing products even though only 12 percent had prior experience with these products.[17]

Individuals and family offices are diverse in their approaches to impact investing. For some, this is a new tool helping them achieve a social or environmental goal, and often it may build on many years of philanthropy, volunteer service, or civic engagement in that area. For others, impact investing is a way of using their wealth to contribute to positive change in the world while generating the income they are looking for. If you find yourself in either of these camps, or are drawn to impact investing for another reason, you're in good company.

Foundations

It was the influence of younger members of the family that prompted the General Service Foundation (GSF) to take an interest in impact investing. Based in Aspen, Colorado, the foundation was created and endowed by Clifton R. Musser and his wife, Margaret Kulp Musser. Most of its trustees are still family members. As with many foundations, new waves of younger board members (which, for this foundation, came in 2005 and 2006) brought with them new ideas, including an interest in impact investing.

Initially, the idea met with skepticism from older board members and from the foundation's adviser, who followed traditional investment orthodoxies. However, with an increasing feeling that its investments should match the foundation's values, the family started looking for a new advisory firm—one that could invest assets with a social impact goal. At the time, such a firm was hard to find. But after coming across Imprint Capital, a San Francisco–based impact investment advisory firm, the foundation decided to have it manage the portion of the endowment it was earmarking for impact investing.

For the foundation, impact investing is something of a balancing act. With a mission to exist in perpetuity, it needs to make competitive returns on its investments. "If we could, we would invest one hundred percent of our assets in impact investing," explains Lani Shaw, the foundation's executive director. "We want to go all the way, but the family also wants the foundation to exist for the next generation."

The foundation made an initial allocation of 10 percent of its endowment to impact investing, which quickly grew to 26%, and is made up largely by private equity investments. This presents a challenge, however, since these investments are locked up for seven to 10 years, while the foundation needs liquidity to make its annual payouts. It is therefore looking to expand its endowment allocation to impact investments while maintaining liquidity and a diversified portfolio.

The approach taken by GSF is an increasingly common one, but is one of many ways in which foundations can engage in impact investing. Other foundations do this by making program-related investments (PRIs). A PRI can advance an organization's mission while also generating a financial return (often, though not always, a below-market return) that can be plowed back into its programs or into other PRIs. PRIs can take a variety of forms—they might be a high-risk or low-interest loan, or an equity investment, in institutions or businesses with social or environmental missions. They could also take the form of deposits in banks that provide loans to low-income populations.

Generally, the use of PRIs is more widespread and has been in existence longer than the practice of using foundation endowments in pursuit of impact. The rationale behind PRIs might include: the desire to recycle philanthropic capital once it has been repaid, to harness larger sources of commercial capital (as Pritzker did for Goldman Sachs, for example), or to act as a bridge enabling social entrepreneurs to transition from grants to commercial capital. At the Rockefeller Foundation, we most often use PRIs to pioneer new investment structures or financial models (such as social impact bonds, which we'll describe in the next chapter) and as leverage for the raising of larger and more commercial sources of capital. Our colleagues at the Bill & Melinda Gates Foundation and the Omidyar Network are creatively using PRIs in similar ways.

The Internal Revenue Service deems PRIs to be charitable. PRIs are a relatively small portion of the impact investing pie, but they are an important one. The KL Felicitas Foundation uses both its endowment and program dollars for impact investments. Motivated by a desire to tackle major problems such as poverty, climate change, and environmental degradation, Charly and Lisa Kleissner set up the foundation to support global social entrepreneurs and enterprises developing innovative ideas, providing them with a variety of services and tools. As such, the foundation takes both a finance-first and an impact-first approach to impact investing. In its finance-first approach, which it uses to preserve its endowment, it looks for investments that advance its mission while preserving capital and generating revenue to support its operations. At the same time, the foundation makes PRIs that provide "social capital" (low-interest financing, loan guarantees, lines of credit, or equity investments with below-market-rate return expectations) to social entrepreneurs and social enterprises. This is the tool that Charly Kleissner used when investing in Healthpoint Services.

Like the KL Felicitas Foundation, an increasing number of foundations are using "both sides of the house" (endowment investments and PRIs) as a means of advancing their mission. The Omidyar Network, established by eBay founder Pierre Omidyar and his wife, Pam, in 2004, has made more than $300 million in impact investments that include concessionary as well as commercial investments.

In addition to making individual investments, the Omidyar Network and the KL Felicitas Foundation are among the relatively small number of foundations that have joined the Rockefeller Foundation in helping to support the growth of the broader field of impact investing. We believe that laying the groundwork for an efficient and effective impact investing industry (through activities such as building networks, supporting the development of impact measurement systems, developing new financial structures, and promoting an enabling policy environment) is one of the most significant ways foundations can advance the field and broaden the overall supply of the resources available to solve social and environmental problems.

Banks

When it comes to the banking sector, efforts to achieve social impact have traditionally taken place through activities that increase financial inclusion. This could be by establishing or investing in microfinance institutions and designing low-entry accounts for first-time customers or by providing financial literacy training. Now, however, some are starting to see the potential in impact investing, both in the context of their own assets and when helping their clients make double-bottom-line investments.

In recent years, most major banks have launched some form of impact investing activity. However, the drivers behind their involvement and the location of impact investing within a bank vary significantly from one institution to the next. For some, impact investing provides a way to comply with regulatory obligations, such as the US Community Reinvestment Act, which encourages banks and savings institutions to provide credit for the places in which they operate, including low-income communities. For others, such as the private banking division of Switzerland-based UBS, it means meeting client interest in Europe and Asia. Meanwhile, J.P. Morgan has a specialized social-sector finance group that originated in its investment banking division but was moved to the corporate US bank. While the group makes investments, arguably its most unique contribution to the field has been through its research products. (The first of these, a report coauthored by J.P. Morgan and the Rockefeller Foundation and titled "Impact Investing: An Emerging Asset Class," is included in the list of resources in the appendix.)

In some cases, tax credits help motivate banks and other institutional investors to make impact investments in areas as diverse as solar energy and community revitalization. In this case, investments in qualifying projects can be exchanged for the federal tax credits associated with the projects. The most widely used tax credit vehicle in impact investing is probably the New Markets Tax Credit Program, which the US Congress established in 2000 to foster investment in businesses and real estate projects in low-income communities. Since its inception, a total of $36.5 billion in tax credit authority (that is, the ability to offer investors tax credits in exchange for equity investments) has been awarded to qualifying community development entities (CDEs) through a competitive application process administered by the US Treasury.

The role of regulation in spurring banks to make impact investing is not limited to the United States. In India, the government's Priority Sector Lending requires banks to set aside a certain portion of their loan portfolios for businesses in "high-impact" sectors. In South Africa, the Broad-Based Black Economic Empowerment (B-BBEE) regulations require banks to lend to black-owned enterprises.

At UBS, on the other hand, impact investing started from within the private bank in response to client interest rather than regulatory or tax incentives. In January 2013 the bank marked the first close of its Impact Investing SME Focus Fund,[18] a fund-of-funds that allows its clients to place capital in a diversified pool of funds serving the world's poorest communities in emerging markets.

Some banks (such as Morgan Stanley's Global Sustainable Finance unit and JPMorgan Chase's social finance unit) have created impact investing units within their corporate structure in order to service multiple bank divisions. In other banks, impact investing activities are located within several units. Citibank, for example, engages in microfinance, community development finance, and energy efficiency finance through different arms of its operations. For these banks, one of the biggest benefits of a defined focus on impact investing may be the ability to link formerly disparate activities that are now considered part of a bigger tent.

Pension Funds and Insurance Companies

As institutional investors, pension funds and insurance companies have a fiduciary duty to produce market-rate returns. Yet more and more of them, driven by a combination of member interest, visionary leadership, and/or regulatory mandate, see social and environmental considerations as part of their fiduciary duty. An increasing number of insurance and pension fund trustees and staff believe that incorporating environmental, social, and governance (ESG) factors into investment strategies will result in better long-term financial performance, or that social or environmental targets can at least be pursued without detracting from competitive returns. Other institutions have taken things a step further and are actively pursuing impact investments designed to create public benefit as well as long-term financial performance. Newark-based Prudential Financial has been making what it now calls social investments since 1976, and currently manages a portfolio of $400 million in this category. In November 2013 the insurance company Zurich made the significant announcement that it would invest $1 billion in green bonds issued by the World Bank and other development finance institutions.[19]

In the case of some pension funds, the impetus to consider social and environmental impact has come from members (pensioners) themselves. TIAA-CREF's investors, for example, have long shown an interest in SRI and related types of investing. In 2006 the firm created a Global Social and Community Investment Group, and the company now manages $14 billion in assets across multiple SRI and social investments portfolios, which span asset classes as well as social and environmental impact. The Service Employees International Union, the fastest-growing union in the United States, launched a capital stewardship unit to do this.

In other cases, regulation has encouraged or required pension funds to target their investments to a particular community or need. In 2011 the South African government passed regulation requiring all pension funds to perform ESG analysis across their portfolios and actively encouraged them to engage in "developmental investing." A number of US states have required public pension funds to engage in "economically targeted investments" (ETIs) that direct investment into underserved communities. In 2001 the Investment Committee at CalPERs, America's largest public pension system, launched the California Initiative with an initial capital commitment of $475 million and the idea of providing attractive investment opportunities by tapping into assets in underserved communities. In 2006, CalPERS made a second allocation, totaling $550 million.[20]

Some pension funds are even making efforts to encourage more institutional investors to embark on impact investing. In the Netherlands, PGGM, which manages €150 billion in health care sector pension assets and has been heavily involved in impact investing, has produced a guide with advice and "how to" suggestions from Tim van der Weide, PGGM's adviser for responsible investment. "Our definition is that our impact investments have to meet regular financial criteria, but at the same time they have to have the intent of societal impact. That is measurable so we can account for the impact to the pension funds whose money we manage and their beneficiaries," he writes. "Our process is that we don't label afterwards, if it is impact investment it needs to be taken into account in the due diligence, because it means we want to measure the societal impact of that investment."[21]

Conclusion

With large as well as small players participating, it is becoming clear that impact investing is no longer a minor actor on the stage of asset management or social impact. Whereas one family office executive described his firm's pioneering role in the industry as "breaking trail for others to follow," a much larger number of people and institutions is now following suit. An Ipsos MORI report conducted in 2011 found that 65 percent of investors with more than £100,000 in investable assets said they wanted to achieve social impact from their investments in addition to financial returns.[22]

The next generation of investors will also play a critical role. Today's young people want to make a difference as well as making money. In a survey by Deloitte of 5,000 Millennials in 18 countries, 71 percent of respondents saw the desire to "improve society" as the top priority of business.[23] Through social media websites and organizations such as Mobilize.org, which empower young people to help solve social problems, the appetite for this generation of individuals to make a difference is clear. And companies report that, increasingly, the questions younger job candidates ask in interviews include those about the organization's commitment to social and environmental issues. This generation is therefore highly likely to want (as impact investors do) to achieve the dual goal of making social impact as well as earning financial returns. And as we mentioned in the introduction, in the next 40 years, some estimate that Generation X and the Millennials could inherit up to $41 trillion from Baby Boomers.

With funds of this size potentially waiting in the wings, the question is whether sufficient numbers of social enterprises and companies exist with the capacity to absorb this investment capital. In the next chapter, we'll take a look at impact enterprises, the different kinds of organizations and funds that make attractive destinations for social impact investments.

CHAPTER 3

Impact Investment Opportunities

E very morning, an hour before the factory opens, the Liberian women who produce garments there gather to pray together for its continued success. This is not required by the company, but is something the women, both Christian and Muslim, do voluntarily because, as shareholders in the company, the success of the enterprise means they can afford health care and education for their families. The fact that the women have jobs at all, however, is thanks to Chid Liberty, a Liberian who grew up in Germany and worked in technology and finance before deciding to return to his native country and set up a social purpose enterprise in Monrovia, the Liberian capital.

To start the company, he raised more than $3 million in funding from private investors and from organizations such as Humanity United, the foundation created by Pam Omidyar with the support of her husband, eBay founder Pierre Omidyar. In 2010, Liberty & Justice started producing Fair Trade–certified clothing and accessories for export to US retailers, providing work and education for Liberian women as well as clean and dignified working conditions.

While Liberia mostly exports raw materials—such as rubber, iron ore, and timber—the Monrovia factory is manufacturing finished goods, which means more of the product value remains in the country. Also, being able to create products gives employees a tremendous sense of pride. "They say, 'We want to show the rest of the world that more than war can come out of Liberia,'" says Liberty. "And to me that's extremely powerful."

Companies such as Liberty & Justice—"impact enterprises," as we call them—offer rich investment opportunities to impact investors. Commercial success is, of course, part of it. Yet equally important is the ability of an enterprise to make a social and environmental impact, in this case transforming lives by combating poverty, conserving natural resources, or empowering workers. Also important is the measurement of social and environmental performance as well as financial targets. For impact enterprises, measurement is part and parcel of reaching their impact goals. This approach, and the challenging environments in which many impact enterprises operate, means it may take them longer to break even than it does their wholly commercial counterparts. But what matters to the impact investor is that social and financial goals are embedded in a company's DNA.

Impact enterprises provide many of the opportunities through which you can match your social and environmental impact with your financial goals. However, other destinations for impact capital are available. In this chapter, we'll look at some of the investment opportunities out there. For while we have so far described impact investing and identified the different types of investors that populate its landscape, to understand how impact investing can be used to bring about positive change in the world, we must look at the different *destinations* for investment capital. These include:

- **Impact enterprises.** These are as diverse as the investors backing them. Some are small-scale social entrepreneurs tackling local problems such as lack of employment opportunities in a marginalized neighborhood. Others have national agendas, with business models that aim to transform the delivery of services such as health care. Their size, operations, customers, products, and services may vary dramatically. They may be looking for debt, equity, or a combination of both. But they have one thing in common: a mission to change the world.
- **Funds.** While some impact investors choose to place their capital directly in individual impact enterprises, an easier route can

be to turn to specialist fund managers who invest their clients' funds in a portfolio of these companies. These funds, which vary widely by sector, geography, size, and investment strategy, are as diverse as the companies they invest in.

- **Real assets.** Physical or tangible assets such as housing developments, forestry, and farmland lend themselves to impact investment since they can be developed so as to promote environmental sustainability, produce employment, or improve livelihoods.

- **Pay-for-performance models.** Also known as social impact bonds (SIBs), these allow investors to invest in proven social services tackling things such as homelessness or poor educational performance. Investors receive returns when an initiative has achieved its intended savings and social or environmental impact.

Impact Enterprises

Impact enterprises are often at the heart of impact investing. These are the companies and entities that pursue social impact and profit by creating jobs, essential goods and services, or environmental benefit. The sources of impact investment capital may be diverse—from individuals to foundations, banks, and institutional investors; from those investing directly to those using funds or other vehicles—but it is impact enterprises that translate this capital into jobs, essential goods and services, or environmental benefit.

These organizations and individuals combine their passion with smart ideas. Take the Indian School Finance Company. ISFC, which was created by impact investing firm Gray Ghost Ventures, helps private schools serving low-income communities in states such as Andhra Pradesh, Karnataka, and Maharashtra to secure credit when they need to make investments such as hiring a new teacher, renting an extra classroom, or purchasing IT equipment. For schools, the loans mean they can offer more places to students, increase the quality of teaching, and introduce new technologies and learning methodologies that create a richer learning experience. Because this helps them attract more students, the schools can become more financially sustainable, which in turn gives them a better chance of securing commercial loans so that they can further scale up their operations. And once the ISFC's loans are repaid, those funds can be recycled to provide loans to other schools. It's a smart model that is financially self-sustaining *and* increases access to education. It is enterprise and impact combined.

Impact enterprises range from those in the earliest stages of development (seed-stage enterprises) to enterprises that have achieved scale or that are operationally stable (growth stage or mature enterprises). The stage of the company you choose to invest in will likely depend on the type of impact you want to have and on the constraints you face. When investing in a small, early-stage enterprise, for example, your funds could have an especially catalytic effect, enabling the enterprise to get off the ground. On the other hand, such companies face much greater rates of failure and may be a long way from being able to return capital to investors. By investing in growth-stage enterprises, you can invest in models with track records of success, which is less risky from a financial and impact standpoint. Investments in mature companies are less likely to be catalytic, however, since such companies are more likely to be able to access capital from other sources.

Impact enterprises not only differ in scale and stage of development, but also in mission and "theory of change." Most obviously, their missions involve making a positive impact on the lives of vulnerable people (social impact), on the planet (environmental impact), or on both. But beyond that, those missions can be pursued through a number of mechanisms. This is what we might call their theory of change. Rather like a business model, a theory of change is a set of steps or a specific strategy that is followed in pursuit of a certain goal. And the models and approaches of impact enterprises (their theories of change) display the same diversity you'd find in the business or nonprofit sectors.

Here are some of the ways in which impact enterprises go about pursuing their social or environmental goals, while also generating revenue or profit:

- **Creating high-quality jobs.** Impact enterprises often make one of their main objectives the creation of good jobs for targeted populations of people, as Liberty & Justice does for women in Liberia. Another example is Greyston Bakery, in the Bronx, New York. Greyston is now famous for baked goods such as the brownies used in Vermont-based Ben & Jerry's ice cream, but it also hires and trains hard-to-employ adults (those with little or no work experience due to former incarceration, drug or alcohol use, poor education, or homelessness). In 2012, Greyston provided employment opportunities and training to 181 local residents.[24]
- **Providing products or services that improve lives.** In India, LifeSpring Hospitals has established small-scale hospitals specializing in low-cost maternity care, providing essential health services to women who would otherwise be unable to access or afford them. By specializing in the most common maternity services (normal deliveries, caesarian sections, and hysterectomies) rather than more complicated procedures, the company has kept investments in technology and equipment low. This allows it to cut costs by being able to standardize processes and reduce the number of certified (and relatively expensive) doctors it needs. Because LifeSpring can offer services that are 30 to 50 percent cheaper than other hospitals, it has become South India's largest chain of maternity hospitals, treating more than 300,000 patients and delivering 18,500 healthy babies.[25]
- **Providing products or services that have a positive impact on the environment.** In Chile, a company called TriCiclos is making it easier for citizens and businesses to recycle and practice sustainability. One way the company has done this is by creating convenient "Clean Collection Points," where 90 percent of household waste can be processed. TriCiclos also creates recycling incentives: For businesses, schools, and other

organizations that contract the company to establish and manage recycling at their facilities, a percentage of the profits from the sale of the recycled materials goes toward the setup and maintenance of that organization's Clean Collection Point.[26]

- **Generating an impact through supply chains.** Oregon-based Sustainable Harvest imports Fair Trade coffee from small-scale farmers in Latin America and East Africa and sells it to large distributors in the United States such as Green Mountain and Peet's Coffee & Tea. Started by David Griswold in 1997, Sustainable Harvest now works with 185,000 farmers in 15 countries.[27] Steady growth in consumer demand for Fair Trade products has enabled a number of newer enterprises to develop businesses that create impact through their supply chains. Maya Mountain Cacao, for example, sources premium cacao from small farmers in Belize and sells it to producers of premium chocolate products. The company provides top-quality cocoa and a substantial income for farmers, while also contributing to reforestation efforts and promoting sustainable organic agricultural practices.

- **Creating replicable models.** Among the goals of Liberty & Justice is the replication of its worker ownership structure and operations by others. Chid Liberty wants the Monrovia factory to become part of a broader network of African apparel factories that meet the same standards, and he wants to spread this model to companies in Asia and Latin America. He stresses the "open source" nature of the company's operations and says it is ready to help others adopt its management practices and collective ownership model—one he believes leads to higher productivity levels and, ultimately, increased profits. This collaborative ethos often distinguishes social enterprises from other for-profit companies. In the mainstream business world, companies almost always want to keep good ideas out of their competitors' hands. But when the goal is to generate social impact as well as profit, many enterprises want to spread their ideas widely so that they can generate impact on a much larger scale.

As you can see, impact enterprises develop distinct business models, or theories of change, to achieve their goals. So as an investor it's important not only to consider whether you want to focus on social impact or on the environment, on enterprises with a narrow impact target or broader goals, on early-stage or mature companies— you may also want to think about the different strategies enterprises use to deliver impact. At the very least, you will want to understand the company's theory of change as part of your due diligence.

Of course, it's not always a case of either/or. While some companies focus their impact on a single intervention (creating local jobs in the Bronx or providing low-cost maternity services in India), in other cases, several of the approaches we've just described coexist within a single company. TriCiclos, for example, strives to generate economic growth alongside recycling, by operating its collection points as franchises that are owned by former waste pickers, often women. In addition, it buys half its supplies locally, thereby helping to stimulate the local economy.

Even when companies focus on tackling a single issue, the complex nature of poverty and social change may mean that their impact is multifaceted. Take Ecotact, a social enterprise that develops solutions to urban challenges. To address lack of clean toilets in slums, it created the Ikotoilet, which combines waterless technology with an innovative business model: costs for operating and cleaning the toilets are covered by selling advertising on the sanitation units, and by offering spaces for other revenue-generating services, such as shoe shines or vendors of cell phone minutes, newspapers, drinks, and snacks.

Most directly, Ecotact—founded by David Kuria, a Kenyan architect with a mission to combat poverty—is providing an essential service in communities where few people have access to a clean toilet. In a country where less than half the population has access to basic sanitation facilities, the impact of this service is hard to underestimate. Ikotoilets bring convenience, privacy, hygiene, and dignity to some of the world's poorest urban communities. But beyond that, as Kuria likes to explain, hygienic sanitation helps lower the incidence of diarrhea, which means it also reduces the malnutrition that accompanies gastrointestinal infections. In this way, the toilets contribute to solving another critical problem: world hunger.

The resources section of our appendix includes more information on the breadth of impact enterprises around the world, and links to organizations that specialize in providing support to these enterprises, such as Ashoka, the Aspen Network of Development Entrepreneurs, and Echoing Green.

Funds

When you are an impact investor, a number of steps lie between you and the people whose lives you hope to help transform. The shortest chain of events occurs when you invest directly in an individual enterprise. But while direct investments are not uncommon, a number of factors—the difficulties of performing due diligence, developing appropriate terms, and managing those investments; and the small size and/or physical distance of many individual investments—lead many impact investors to place their capital with specialist fund managers who in turn invest in a portfolio of businesses.

In most cases, your investment in a fund will resemble the investments a limited partner (LP) makes into a general partner (GP) in traditional investing—you will pay a management fee, and any profit generated by the underlying investments will accrue to you and the GP according to a predetermined formula. The funds, however, are as diverse as the enterprises they invest in. Among the factors that distinguish the various funds are:

- **Their mission, including how broad or targeted their focus is by sector or geography.** For example, LeapFrog Investments (whose first fund was a $135 million vehicle[28]) has a primary focus on micro-insurance, or the provision of insurance services to communities that lack access to them, in a number of emerging markets. Meanwhile, in the United States, Boston Community Capital, the holding company for a diverse set of community investment funds, has provided over $920 million for investments in things that revitalize low-income neighborhoods, such as affordable housing, child care facilities, and solar energy.[29] Unlike LeapFrog, Boston Community Capital is diverse by sector but has a primary focus on the greater Boston area. It describes its approach as looking "beyond the standard metrics of collateral and credit history, instead basing loans on our assessment of the borrower's capabilities, knowledge of the community and our evaluation of each project's impact."[30]

- **The stage of company or the type of asset they invest in, and the type of capital they provide (such as debt or equity).** In India, Aavishkaar, a fund manager, aims to improve the livelihoods of rural communities by identifying early-stage entrepreneurial ventures in farming regions and finding limited partners prepared to provide "patient capital," equity investments that contribute to human development while achieving near-commercial returns over a longer period than traditional investments. Using these investments, Aavishkaar provides rural enterprises with initial risk capital and support in the strategy, operations, and networking needed for these businesses to expand. Aavishkaar also aims to demonstrate to mainstream venture capitalists the potential for this kind of investment.[31] In contrast, private equity investor Abraaj Capital invests in more mature companies across Asia, Africa, Latin America, and the Middle East that have already demonstrated a track record. Still other funds provide debt rather than equity and/or invest in assets other than enterprises.

- **The level of financial return they target.** LeapFrog and Aavishkaar both advertise to investors a rate of return that is competitive for mainstream investments of a similar risk profile. Root Capital, in contrast, does not. It provides loans as well as technical assistance to cooperatives of farmers in Africa and

Latin America. Its loans are made less risky by the staff's expertise in agricultural lending and in its use of advance purchase contracts from large importers of Fairtrade commodities (such as Starbucks) as collateral. However, the costs of serving Root's target clients mean that it cannot provide a market rate of return to its investors. It provides a 2 percent return on notes that range from one to five years.

- **Arrangements that resemble the investments a limited partner (LP) makes into a general partner (GP) in traditional investing.** In Brazil, Vox Capital, the country's first impact investing fund, serves low-income communities through a portfolio of high-potential businesses working in financial services, affordable development, health, and education. Vox looks like a traditional general partnership, but it has adapted its approach to the types of companies it invests in: it ties the profits of the manager to its impact ratings, it is commissioning an annual social audit, and it expects to invest 3 percent of fund assets in small, high-risk investments in companies that have graduated from a well-regarded social business incubator. Structured as "convertible notes," most of these debt investments are likely to be written off, but Vox hopes to convert a few of them into equity. By the end of 2013, Vox Capital had raised over $35 million in its 10-year equity fund.

- **Funds targeting particular socioeconomic groups.** In the United States, Jalia Ventures' Impact America Fund provides seed- and expansion-stage capital to companies owned by entrepreneurs of color that have a social or environmental mission, particularly those that seek to benefit underserved US communities. The fund's investments include Red Rabbit, a Harlem-based company that provides healthy and locally sourced school meals and snacks to urban school districts. Funds that target vulnerable socioeconomic groups are not specific to the United States and can be found around the world.

- **Funds focused on companies that cut across multiple sectors and geographies.** Launched in 2012, the Small Enterprise Impact Investing Fund (SEIIF) focuses on small- and medium-size businesses in developing countries but offers investors diversity in terms of models, geographies, and activities. The fund (managed by Symbiotics, an investment boutique specializing in emerging, sustainable, and inclusive finance, and advised by Oxfam, the antipoverty charity) aims to raise $100 million in three years, which will be invested in a portfolio of debt and equity instruments focusing on those with low-risk, high-impact profiles. The financial goals for SEIIF are capital preservation and the yielding of a realistic return for investors.[32]

A fund manager might provide debt, equity, or a combination of the two to companies at varying stages of maturity. And as with traditional investments, fund investment strategies allow for varying appetites for risk. In impact investing, funds also differ in the relative priority of impact and financial return. You can get an idea of the number and diversity of funds on the ImpactBase website, which hosts a database of dedicated impact investment fund managers. As of December 31, 2013, the site contained profiles of 279 funds.

Funds often play a critical role in closing the gap between an investor and the ultimate destination for his or her capital, but there are limitations to the use of fund structures in impact investing. The traditional 2/20 structure for equity investments (typically an annual management fee of around 2 percent of assets, an annual performance fee around 20 percent of profits, and an exit in approximately seven years) is often recreated in this sector, but it may not work for a lot of the companies targeted by impact investors.

For one thing, a 2 percent management fee, particularly for a smaller fund, is unlikely to enable the type of business support and technical assistance many impact enterprises require. The time horizon for these funds often leads them to seek an exit at a time that does not serve the investors or companies. In addition, many fund managers are compensated solely through participation in profit sharing, despite the fact that their funds generally have nonfinancial as well as financial objectives.

While innovation at the fund level remains arguably too rare, some promising models are leading the way. Brazil's Vox Capital, for example, has adapted its approach through features such as Vox Labs, which supports potential Vox investees that are in their seed phase, and a profit-sharing formula for the general partner that depends on social as well as financial performance. Some funds have raised "sidecar" facilities alongside the fund's investment capital that provide technical assistance to their pipeline and portfolio companies.

Other investors have found creative ways to arrange for a mission-aligned exit. For example, SJF Ventures (a North Carolina–based fund manager making venture investments in resource efficiency, sustainability, and technology-enhanced service sectors) arranged an exit from portfolio company CleanScapes (a Seattle-based waste management and recycling company) when the latter was sold in 2011 to a mission-aligned company called Recology. An employee-owned, San Francisco–based waste management company with a mission to produce zero waste, Recology presented both the best financial offer and an ideal opportunity to maintain the mission of CleanScapes. Other fund managers have sought exits by selling to other mission-aligned investors or arranging a gradual sale to company management or employees. As the impact investing industry evolves, the hope is that these types of models can proliferate.

Real Assets

In addition to direct investments, or investments in debt or equity funds, impact investments may fall into the category known in mainstream investing as "real assets." Many of these investments (from forests and farmland to affordable residential developments) are larger and therefore more likely candidates for institutional rather than individual investors.

The first social purpose real estate fund in the United States was launched in 2012 with investors including Citi, Morgan Stanley, Prudential Financial, Inc., the John D. and Catherine T. MacArthur Foundation, and the Ford Foundation. Called the Housing Partnership Equity Trust, it works with 12 leading nonprofit housing providers across the country to acquire apartment buildings that provide quality rental homes for families, seniors, and others with modest incomes. Each participant in the trust benefited from the others' respective strengths. Without capital that was ready to go, the nonprofit housing providers found they often lost out to commercial housing developers, especially in competitive urban markets. And without the combined expertise of these providers, co-investors would not have been able to deploy their capital to improve the lives of people in low-income communities.

While rent is usually the biggest expense for modest-income families, affordable rental housing is far from their only need. In 2013 in Baltimore, a "transit-oriented development" project called Center/West (mixed-use residential and commercial areas designed to maximize access to public transport) received a $2 million preconstruction investment from 5 Stone Green Capital, a "green" clean-tech real estate fund that raises money from pension funds and institutional investors for environmentally sustainable, energy-efficient, technologically smart commercial real estate investments. Center/West focuses on the overall economic potential of the area and seeks to help rejuvenate a neighborhood that has long been designated an "urban renewal area." Located a quarter mile from Baltimore's Inner Harbor, when fully developed, the mixed-use and LEED-certified project[33] will include affordable housing, a school, and retail outlets with a "green grocer" as anchor tenant, and will create local job opportunities, all within buildings whose construction emphasizes sustainable design principles and energy/water efficiency.

Real assets can also be particularly appealing if you have a strong orientation toward environmental impact, as they include renewable energy, forestry, and other natural resource investments. The Lyme Timber Company, as mentioned earlier, a private timberland investment management organization, focuses on the acquisition and sustainable management of land with unique conservation value. The company's current portfolio includes 475,000 acres of forestland in Delaware, Louisiana, Maine, Massachusetts, New York, South Carolina, Tennessee, Virginia, and Wisconsin.[34]

Real assets are not necessarily available to all investors. Lyme Timber is recommended by Cambridge Associates, a mainstream financial advisory firm, to clients looking for impact investments, but it is available only to accredited investors. However, the Nature Conservancy recently developed a Conservation Note, a financial product that enables retail investors to invest as little as $25,000 in programs that conserve natural areas and essential resources, help protect wildlife, restore drinking water supplies, and improve people's lives.[35]

Pay-for-Performance Models

While some impact investments might seem familiar to traditional investors, new vehicles are emerging that look completely different. One new financing model gaining support among impact investors is based on the concept of paying social service agencies (not generally considered destinations for investment) for performance. This is often referred to as a social impact bond (SIB), or a pay-for-success bond. Our colleagues at the Rockefeller Foundation have played a significant role in supporting the development and take-up of this innovative form of impact investing.

Despite the name, SIBs do not resemble traditional bonds. Instead, they harness private capital to fund programs that improve lives while also saving governments' money, with a portion of the savings to the government used to repay the investors. One example is the

J.B. Pritzker/Goldman Sachs SIB, which invested in early childhood education in Utah, thereby improving educational outcomes while reducing the costs to governments incurred from grade repetition and tutoring.

Here's how it works. When a local authority or department has identified a successful intervention to address a problem—from long-term unemployment or homelessness to poor student performance at government schools—it enters a contractual agreement with an investor or an intermediary (such as a bank or a foundation) that can raise funds from other investors. Well-proven service providers execute the program. And as soon as the terms of the contract are met (as assessed by independent evaluators) and the project has achieved its intended savings and social or environmental impact, returns are paid out to investors.

As governments struggle to address persistent social problems with increasingly stretched public finances, this pay-for-performance approach is an appealing one. First, tapping into private capital strips out some of the risks of making investments with taxpayer dollars. And by replacing tax dollars with investment funds, those tax dollars can be freed up for use in other services or preventive programs the governments might otherwise not be able to offer.

The model can guarantee a supply of long-term investment capital, protecting social programs from the funding ebbs and flows that accompany changes in political leadership or the changing interests of donors. While paying by results is not new, traditionally it has been service providers receiving payment for performance—which brings with it other challenges, as not all small providers can take on the costs or the risks of not receiving payment. Because the pay-for-performance model provides up-front funding for executing the programs, service providers can be confident of being paid.

The first SIB was developed by former investment bankers David Hutchison and Toby Eccles at Social Finance UK, chaired by well-known venture capitalist Sir Ronald Cohen, and pioneered by the UK government in the eastern British city of Peterborough in 2010.

The investment, which closed at £5 million,[36] paid for a team of counselors to use a well-proven approach to working with short-sentence inmates (those with custodial sentences of less than 12 months) about to leave Peterborough prison. Those prisoners who were mentored, given job training, and connected with services (both before and after leaving prison) were less likely to reoffend.[37] This would provide savings to the government in the form of the money it would take to place the prisoners back into incarceration. (Currently about 60 percent of the adults on short-term sentences will reoffend within a year of release.[38]) Once an observable change in recidivism occurred, the Ministry of Justice would pay investors back at market rates.

Early evidence suggests the SIB is showing promise. If reoffending drops by 7.5 percent or more, investors will receive a share of the government's long-term savings.[39] The return increases as the reduction in the reoffending rate exceeds the 7.5 percent goal, up to a maximum of 13 percent paid to investors, with the total Ministry of Justice payout capped at £8 million.[40]

In the United Kingdom, the model is being adopted rapidly, with 13 SIBs up and running in 2013 or contracts signed (up from just one in 2011) and more than 40 social-sector organizations involved.[41] Other countries are beginning to build up their own SIB ecosystems, including Australia and the United States, where several are already underway. In his 2014 budget, President Barack Obama proposed a $300 million fund to help states and local governments establish their own "pay for success" programs, and at the end of 2013, New York became the first state to lead its own SIB, focused on recidivism.

And while foundations have been early investors in social impact bonds, individual investors and some funds are now showing interest in the model.

For investors, this approach holds some risk: they receive no return on their investment if the program or intervention fails. However, it is appealing because it links social impact with financial return—success translates directly into payments.

So far, pay-for-performance investments have been flowing largely into public-sector projects such as prison recidivism prevention or enhanced education. However, the model could be adapted to meet other challenges. For example, a social impact bond might be structured to pay for improved health care in developing countries or logistics systems that would enable international relief agencies to reduce the cost of delivering emergency supplies to communities hit by famine, natural disaster, conflict, or disease.

Some investors are starting to look at these possibilities. The Center for Global Development and the UK-based organization Social Finance are currently exploring the potential for development impact bonds (DIBs) to secure private investor funding for development programs, with international donors or host country governments paying for performance. It is too early to tell if and how soon DIBs will emerge as a credible source of development finance. But as governments, development agencies, and others look for ways to do more with less, innovative financial instruments will enable successful social interventions to achieve scale and precious public dollars to stretch farther.

Conclusion

The range of investment opportunities available to impact investors is broad and growing. Such opportunities are diverse by impact objective, asset class, and return expectation, and by many other parameters. Unquestionably, these opportunities are greater in number and quality than they were five years ago. With the growth of the community of impact investors comes a new question, however. Are there enough impact enterprises out there to absorb this new mission-driven investment capital? The danger some see is that if the supply is insufficient, money might find its way into too many enterprises that ultimately fail, in turn creating the risk that impact investing itself might be deemed a failure. Alternatively, investors might become frustrated and give up when they do not find a ready supply of investable opportunities.

However, others say there is a strong pipeline of investments. Some believe that any perceived lack of supply stems from a disconnect between investors and investment opportunities. "The global impact investment market includes diverse investment opportunities and investors with a wide range of interests," says Amit Bouri, managing director of the Global Impact Investing Network (GIIN). "While people debate whether the market has too much capital or too many deals, it is clear that the current market isn't clearing efficiently—capital and deals aren't connecting the way they need to be. This is a characteristic of a young market."

We believe that the balance of supply and demand for impact investing capital varies by region, sector, and stage of enterprise, as well as the particular requirements of a given investor. The picture looks different, for example, for early-stage capital than for growth-stage capital: a 2013 survey of investors conducted by J.P. Morgan and the GIIN highlights the disproportionate percentage of capital that is seeking to be placed in mature versus young companies.[42]

In addition, the picture may look different to those who are able or willing to put in the work needed to structure a good deal. Investable deals can often be generated if investors are prepared to apply some elbow grease. When, for example, the Heron Foundation wanted to use its endowment to make liquid investments in small businesses in low-income or minority neighborhoods, it found no opportunities that would provide the financial and impact returns as well as the liquidity it was seeking. Rather than give up, the foundation worked with Community Capital Management (which manages impact investing portfolios of government-related bonds issued to promote community development) and the Small Business Administration (SBA) to use information such as census data to identify businesses operating in low- and moderate-income communities and to create customized pools of SBA loans for institutional investors.

All parties benefited. For the SBA, this increased the number of investors interested in making loans to small businesses and entrepreneurs. Community Capital Management could access a broader range of investment opportunities for its clients. The companies selling the loans could expand their market. And by being able to target its fixed-income investments, Heron could allocate more capital in pursuit of its goals.[43]

As the Heron example demonstrates, impact investments can come together if investors are prepared to be innovative and work collaboratively. Debra Schwartz, director of program-related investments at the John D. and Catherine T. MacArthur Foundation, put it eloquently: "Impact investments are made, not found."[44] For investors willing and able to roll up their sleeves, the sky may be the limit.

What is not up for debate, however, is the fact that for impact investing to bring about social change, both sides of the investment equation are needed: a robust supply of capital and a sufficient number of investable enterprises. While impact investors provide the capital, it is these enterprises that can turn that capital into innovative products or create financially sustainable business models that deliver everything from health care and education to clean energy and forest conservation.

Of course, assessing the social or environmental (as well as financial) performance of these investments can be complex. To advance impact investing, therefore, robust measurement systems are essential. After all, smart investors would demand detailed feedback on the for-profit companies in which they invested—as an impact investor, you should assess your investments with the same rigor. In the next chapter we will analyze the role of measurement systems in impact investing. And we will look at other factors (such as policy frameworks and information systems) that are needed to underpin the impact investing industry and support its growth.

CHAPTER 4

Support Systems

By installing its own water infrastructure in new housing developments, Mexico-based Agua Natural en Red is delivering affordable purified water directly to its clients, saving them not only money but also time and space by eliminating the need to buy and store water containers. The system has environmental sustainability benefits as well, since the bottled water trucks driving through the streets in Mexican cities contribute to increased carbon emissions, while the plastic water containers they deliver generate waste.[45] The company is clearly contributing to solving both social and environmental challenges. But how do you measure the impact of a company such as Agua Natural en Red? This is a critical question for any impact investor. For if impact investing is to fulfill its dual nature—delivering both profits and social or environmental impact— you need to be able to measure both these returns on investment.

The Agua Natural en Red example illustrates two important and related developments in the evolution of impact investing's market infrastructure: measurement and certification systems. The company is part of the portfolio of IGNIA, a Mexico-based impact investing venture capital fund. IGNIA is a "Pioneer Fund" participating in an early version of the Global Impact Investing Rating System (GIIRS), which provides comparable and transparent social and environmental performance data on enterprises seeking investment capital.[46] Meanwhile, IGNIA is also a Certified B Corporation, which means it has met B Lab's high standards of social and environmental performance, legal accountability, and transparency.

Of course, as anyone familiar with the investment and finance sector knows, measuring returns is a complex business. It took decades for the traditional financial sector to develop robust ratings and reporting systems, and even then, there remains room for improvement. Add in the assessment of social and environmental returns, and the complexities increase dramatically. While it's one thing to count the dollars, it is another to put hard numbers on the returns to society of improved health care or the value of a healthy tropical forest. Take water provision—when investing in this essential human and natural resource, would you want to see your returns measured by the number of people served, the volume of water delivered, the lower disease rates resulting from access to clean water, or the improved viability of local rivers and watersheds?

The good news is that much work is being done on developing the kinds of systems needed to help you, as an investor, gain a clearer picture of how your money is being put to work and the impact it is making. In addition, certification and legal systems have emerged that make it easier to identify the investments likely to make and sustain the kind of impact you're looking for. At the same time, policy makers are introducing measures (whether by offering investors tax incentives or financing the development of an ecosystem of investment fund managers and other intermediaries) that will help attract more people and organizations to impact investing by fostering the growth of robust market infrastructure.

The ability to measure impact investments is among several pieces of scaffolding needed to support the growth of the impact investment sector. In fact, assessment and rating systems are among the most important tools for impact investors. Here's what we see as the critical elements of this support system that you, as a current or prospective impact investor, should be looking for:

- **Data on financial performance.** The industry is growing and attracting more investors because it is building up the kind of robust data on the realized financial and impact performance of investments and funds that is available in traditional investing.

- **Impact performance measurement.** If the practice of using investments to pursue social and environmental impact as well as profit is to become more broadly adopted, that impact needs to be measurable. As with certification and legal registration (see next bullet point), these systems provide an easy impact screen for investors and others who may not be ready for in-depth impact analysis or want to do all the measurement legwork.

- **Certification and legal registration.** Certifications (such as the B Corp system) that demand rigorous assessment processes and higher levels of legal accountability can give investors confidence in the performance, risk mitigation, and practices of impact enterprises. In addition, a new corporate form, the "benefit corporation," is taking rating systems one step further by legally enabling and requiring companies to pursue their social and environmental missions as well as creating traditional shareholder value.

- **Policy measures.** Governments play a critical role in creating the kinds of policies that will encourage the growth of the impact investing industry. These measures increase market transparency, make it easier for you to participate, and enhance your choices as an investor.

Data on Financial Performance

In 2011, J.P. Morgan and GIIN conducted a survey of impact investors to gather information on their activities and perspectives on the future of the sector. One question asked investors to identify the greatest barriers to industry growth. The most common response? A lack of data on prior performance.[47] This is hardly surprising. After all, when you make any investment, one of the key questions is "Does the past performance of this fund manager give me any indication that my investment is likely to deliver returns in the future?" The standard disclaimer that "past performance is no guarantee of future results" is just as relevant for your impact investments as it is for more traditional investments, but the reality remains that a fund manager's track record is likely to be a significant factor in most of your investment decisions.

Data on the performance of companies and funds help give you confidence that promised financial and impact returns may be achievable. Jean Case, philanthropist and former senior executive at AOL, asserts that "as impact investing matures, data on the size of market, risks, benefits, and return on investment by asset class is critical for the market to scale and move forward. Hard data on financial returns and measurable social impacts will clarify risks and opportunities needed to attract new investors into the field, likely expand both capital and deal flow as a result, and help to scale this important movement that holds such great promise."

Case is not alone in her belief that performance data are critical to the development of the field. In its 2013 report on impact investing, the World Economic Forum's main recommendations for moving impact investing into the mainstream were not only to create a system for tracking and reporting social and environmental impact but also to increase the transparency of realized financial returns.[48]

Unfortunately, there's no shortcut when it comes to past performance. Many of the funds that are most visible in the impact investing space—those listed on the GIIN's ImpactBase platform, for example—are relatively new funds that are or have recently been raising capital. Over time, data on the financial performance of these funds will start to accumulate. But in the meantime, more needs to be done to fill the information gap. The GIIN is planning to undertake dedicated research on the realized performance of impact investing funds, and others are considering related initiatives.

Some pioneering fund managers, such as Bridges Ventures in the UK or global microfinance fund MicroVest, have been in the market long enough to have established track records. A few pioneering investors, such as the KL Felicitas Foundation,[49] are prepared to share the data they have amassed over many years, as are investor networks such as Investors' Circle, an angel network, which shares details of its investments, including those that have resulted in exits.[50] Others are performing their own internal analyses. Prudential Financial, which has managed a $400 million portfolio of community and impact investments for more than 30 years, benchmarked the returns on that portfolio against a comparable high-yield index at the end of 2013. In a low-interest-rate environment, its community impact investments beat the high-yield index benchmark, which gives the company's management greater confidence in impact investing.

Data on investments that have failed, on the other hand, are perhaps more valuable than data on positive track records—though investors are less likely to want to share those stories, and understandably so. Some worry that there is a double standard with regard to impact investments, and that they will be held to a higher bar than mainstream investments. Of course, it's essential to keep in mind that investing is difficult across the board and that mainstream investments often underperform or fail. But in the absence of a fast-forward button, the open sharing of information about successes, failures, and lessons learned will help both investors and companies spend less time reinventing the wheel and more time scaling up models that work.

Impact Performance Measurement

Of all the support mechanisms you need for successful impact investing, impact rating and measurement systems are among the most critical. The ability to assess the social and environmental returns of a given investment as well as the financial returns allows you to differentiate between degrees of impact and to monitor the dual performance of your investment over time. While this is challenging, given the complexities of measuring things such as improvements in education systems or better access to clean water, it is by no means impossible. And impact measurement and management systems play a critical role in helping you distinguish good companies from good marketing, enabling you (and fund managers and others) to judge performance and make informed decisions.

Of course, measuring social or environmental impact across different enterprises is extremely complicated, even when you are comparing potential investments in companies of the same size, sector, or impact objective. Local conditions, whether cultural, infrastructural, political, or environmental, can affect both the impact being made by the company you're investing in and the way that company decides to develop its products and services. So if you're trying to compare the impact of a low-cost maternity hospital in India with one in Argentina, this might prove extremely difficult.

Moreover, in order to compare and benchmark the impact that companies have made on everything from food security and water conservation to increased access to education, you need to be able to rely on agreed-upon basic definitions. Say you're comparing the performance of two companies creating products for low-income communities. What does "low-income" actually mean in different parts of the world? In order to make meaningful conclusions, there is a need to compare like with like.

Many efforts have been made over the years to develop measurement systems that can assess social and environmental performance, but until recently few such systems have been tailored to the broad universe of impact investments. Most of them have been either sector-specific, such as the tools that have emerged to assess the performance of microfinance institutions, or focused on assessing the environmental, social, and governance (ESG) performance of large companies. Fortunately, new measurement tools and systems have been developed over the past five years to meet the specific needs of impact investors.

A New Rating System

It was because of the lack of measurement systems specifically designed for impact investing that B Lab,[51] a Pennsylvania-based nonprofit, developed the Global Impact Investing Rating System (GIIRS). With funding from the Rockefeller Foundation, B Lab developed a comprehensive and transparent ratings system for assessing companies and funds on their social and environmental impact. The idea was to provide a tool to help not only mission-driven investors and fund managers but also entrepreneurs and companies to measure and improve the way they served customers, workers, and communities.

Essentially, the GIIRS approach is similar to that of Morningstar's investment rankings or S&P's credit risk ratings, but it is applied to the ranking of enterprises and funds on their social and environmental performance. Here's how it works:

- Companies are assessed using 50 to 120 weighted questions divided into four impact areas (governance, workers, community, and environment), each containing several subcategories of questions.
- While social and environmental impact areas are a constant, the system also enables more nuanced assessments of how a company may make its impact.
- In addition, a company's industry and its "impact business model" (that is, the way it seeks to have impact) affect how much weighting is given to that impact area. For example, a company whose impact is achieved through employing marginalized workers would have its "employee" score weighted more heavily in its overall score. An enterprise focusing on manufacturing (that is, one more likely to have greater environmental impact than a service provider) would be asked specific questions related to its environmental policies, practices, and impact, and these would be weighted more heavily. And so forth.

As an investor or fund manager, you can use GIIRS to compare impact investments across geographies, sectors, industries, and sizes. And a growing number of organizations have declared an investment preference for GIIRS-rated funds or companies in their impact strategies. Among them are what GIIRS calls its "Pioneer Investors," which include family offices; social finance organizations; global financial institutions such as J.P. Morgan and UBS; institutional investors such as Prudential; and foundations such as the W.K. Kellogg Foundation and the Skoll Foundation.

It is not just funds such as IGNIA that use GIIRS. UBS, the global bank based in Switzerland, is another. In response to growing demand from clients, the bank's Values-Based Investing unit raised a fund-of-funds (which offers investors additional diversification by spreading money across multiple companies and multiple fund managers) that will provide finance to small and medium-size enterprises in emerging markets. To give investors confidence in the fund's ability to deliver tangible and measurable social and environmental impact, UBS realized it needed to offer evidence in the form of a rating for the impact of its investment product. So the bank turned to the GIIRS rating system to assess its fund managers and started using the B Analytics data platform (which enables investors to access, benchmark, and analyze a range of impact data in one place) to collect and analyze all the data from underlying companies. It then worked with Deloitte, the advisory firm, to implement a robust data verification process.[52]

If you are an investor working from within a large institution such as a bank or pension fund, rating systems are critical for helping you fulfill your fiduciary duty and may offer your clients greater confidence in the impact investment products you are providing them.

A Taxonomy for Impact

The need for apples-to-apples impact comparison and industry benchmarks has driven the development of another critical piece of industry infrastructure: a set of common terms that can be used to describe a range of impacts. Impact Reporting and Investment Standards (IRIS), created with start-up funding from the Rockefeller Foundation and others, has developed and maintains a database of standardized definitions. IRIS, which is run by GIIN, provides a taxonomy and common set of definitions for describing social and environmental performance. You can access this information on the website.[53] So when looking at, say, clean energy companies developing systems or products to reduce emissions, investors can identify industry-standard metrics for reporting and measuring those companies' environmental performance. Once similar companies are measuring their impact in the same way, they can be meaningfully compared with one another, or tracked over time, or used to benchmark performance in their sector.

With a role similar to that of the FASB (Financial Accounting Standards Board) and GAAP (generally accepted accounting principles), IRIS is continually refining its database of terms. It also offers a range of tools to help you get started in tracking, measuring, and managing the impact of your investments. And by providing a common set of definitions, it allows anyone providing market infrastructure (e.g., GIIRS) to speak the same language.

No One Size Fits All

While GIIRS and IRIS are emerging as leading tools, the quest to find the perfect means of rating social and environmental impact is not over. Both tools have been evolving to meet the demands of the market, and will almost certainly be joined by additional systems over time. For example, IRIS has developed a number of resources to help users navigate its detailed taxonomy of terms, but some still prefer an off-the-shelf solution that requires less customization. Others see rating systems such as GIIRS as too comprehensive and prescriptive, and as unable to capture sufficiently the nuances of the investments they are making. The B Lab team has been emphasizing the flexibility of its data platform, B Analytics, for those who are not yet ready to get their portfolios rated or who want more than is contained in a rating. Ultimately, however, assessing social and environmental impact often involves value judgments that are difficult to capture in hard data alone.

Other systems have emerged along the way. For example, Pulse (initially developed by Acumen Fund and later absorbed by B Analytics) is a data management platform free to nonprofits that allows the impact of different projects to be compared. A system called social return on investment, or SROI, puts a dollar valuation on social and environmental outcomes in the impact investing space. Meanwhile, firms such as FTSE4Good, in the United Kingdom, and MCSI, a US provider of investment decision support tools, rank larger companies on their ESG (environmental, social, and governance) performance. These firms produce research and indices that may provide valuable input for your investment decisions, particularly if they lie on the SRI side of the impact investing spectrum. Also of interest to SRI investors may be reporting standards such as the Global Reporting Initiative (GRI), which provides companies with guidelines for measuring and reporting their social and environmental performance, and the Carbon Disclosure Project, which works with hundreds of institutional investors to collect data specifically on companies' environmental impact, including companies' carbon emissions and consumption of water and other natural resources.

The impact enterprises you're investing in may even find that IRIS and GIIRS are not perfectly suited to the business models they've developed, since businesses are often highly dependent on their local or sectoral context. Some impact enterprises might therefore prefer a more flexible analytics system that allows them to track the things they're most concerned about.

As an investor, you must decide whether these metrics are adequate for your particular goals and will allow you to make comparisons between the performance of your investment and that of other companies—or whether you need to undertake more qualitative forms of due diligence and interact personally with the companies you're investing in.

Debates over the best way to measure impact enterprises and funds will continue, and competing systems may (and should) emerge. But however measurement standards evolve, one thing is clear: to be an effective impact investor, you need such standards.

And while, for now, GIIRS and the B Analytics data platform are the main tools available to you, their creators foresee a day when others will enter the market and give impact investors the kind of choice that mainstream investors now enjoy.

Certification and Legal Form

"It's time for a fresh approach to our kids' nutrition," say Kristin Richmond and Kirsten Tobey, cofounders of Oakland-based Revolution Foods, a company whose mission is to build lifelong healthy eaters by making "kid-inspired, chef-crafted" food accessible to everyone. The way they do this, they explain, is by "revolutionizing" the food available at stores and schools, particularly in low-income communities. Every day, from local kitchens, the company prepares healthy meals using natural ingredients free of high-fructose corn syrup, artificial colors and flavors, and preservatives and delivers those meals to schools, with at times all costs covered by the federal school lunch reimbursement program. The two founders link the health of children and the health of the nation. "There were a lot of great efforts going on in education reform—but no one was paying attention to what we were feeding kids at school and how that sets them up for success," says Tobey. Since it started in 2006 as a small operation serving 300 meals a day, the company has expanded rapidly. Revolution Foods now delivers more than a million fresh, healthy meals each week to schools across the United States and distributes convenient, natural "Meal Kits" to retailers across the nation.

The year 2011 marked a milestone for Revolution Foods—that was when B Lab certified it as a B Corporation, demonstrating that it had met rigorous standards of social and environmental performance, legal accountability, and transparency; and providing potential investors with robust evidence that the company was creating impact. In doing so, it joined hundreds of Certified B Corps (by 2014 there were more than 900 in 29 countries). Once certified, these companies can tap into B Lab's portfolio of services and support. A sister organization, Sistema B, is running a similar program in Latin America through which companies can become certified as "Empresa B" organizations. And as discussed later in this chapter, legislation now allows companies in many places to register as a new type of business entity: a benefit corporation.

Certification

For impact enterprises such as Revolution Foods, B Corp certification has several advantages. It can have operational benefits. For Revolution Foods, this includes obtaining discounted prices from certain vendors. And by distinguishing the company, it can help build trust, and pride, among staff and customers (stakeholders that are critical to the success of a high-impact business). In addition, because B Corp certification includes a legal requirement that a company expand its fiduciary duty to consider stakeholders, not just shareholders, it puts the founders' mission into the legal DNA of the business, making it more likely that its values will survive new investors, new owners, and new management as the company grows. Here's how the certification process works:

- First, companies take the B Impact Assessment, which looks at the company's overall impact on all its stakeholders (workers, consumers, community, environment), accounting both for the underlying model the company uses to create impact and for its environmental, social, and governance practices.
- Then a B Lab staff member conducts an assessment review over the phone to go over any questions that were unclear or difficult to answer, and accounting for factors and practices that are unique to the given company. On the assessment review, eight to 12 high-value questions from the B Impact Assessment are randomly selected, and the company is asked to demonstrate these practices in detail through documentation.
- Finally, a disclosure questionnaire allows the company to disclose confidentially any sensitive practices, fines, or sanctions related

to it or its partners. While this does not affect the company's rating, more detail might be requested, if necessary.

- As a further measure of verification, one in five B Corps are randomly selected for an onsite audit during their two-year license terms.

The B Impact Assessment only measures a company's social and environmental impact at one point in time. So to give companies a better chance of maintaining their mission as they grow (when raising third-party capital or going through an IPO or sale) Certified B Corps are also required to expand their fiduciary duties to include consideration of their stakeholders. In many places, this simply means amending their existing corporate documents to include standard language (published on B Lab's website) to state that when making operating and liquidity decisions, officers and directors "shall consider" the impact of their decisions on all stakeholders, not just shareholders.

This combination of higher performance and legal standards provides a robust way of demonstrating a company's commitment to its social mission. "There's that third party validation," agrees Kirsten Tobey. "We've always adhered to our core values, but it gives us that stamp of approval that says this is legit."

By giving this "stamp of approval," certification provides an important tool for impact investors. Whether you're an individual investor or fund manager, certification is a sign that the impact enterprises you're considering investing in have been through a rigorous assessment of their practices and that they can be held accountable for maintaining their mission.

Legal Form

Another mechanism that can give you this confidence is recent legislation allowing the creation of a new type of legal corporate entity. In a growing number of US states, the ability to register as a benefit corporation is helping companies bake their social and environmental missions into their operations. A benefit corporation is a business entity (like a C Corp, S Corp, LLC, or other legal form) that requires those running it to pursue public benefit and to consider the interests of all stakeholders (community, workers, and the environment) as well as shareholders (and to report annually on how they have had a "material positive impact" on society). While benefit corporations may also pursue B Corp certification in order to have a third-party seal of approval, this is not a registration requirement of the legislation.

Like certification, benefit corporation registration confers a stamp of approval on a company, and that can give you as an impact investor confidence to make an investment in that company. However, when investing in a benefit corporation, you gain an additional assurance: that its legal structure will preserve the company's mission in the case of a sale. In many jurisdictions, traditional corporations looking for a buyer are legally bound to accept the highest offer. By contrast, in the sale process for a benefit corporation, directors must focus on maintaining the social and environmental goals of the company and can require a buyer to make commitments to the mission. So if you're investing for the long term, the benefit corporation's legal structure assures you that the mission that originally provided the motive for your investment will not be abandoned.

This is why Liberty & Justice, which is currently a C Corporation, is considering reregistering as a benefit corporation. While Chid Liberty sees risks in this (including deterring mainstream investors who may be unfamiliar with the benefit corporation structure or who worry about extra layers of due diligence), he notes that a big advantage of the legislation is in the ability of a benefit corporation to turn down a buyer that might, for example, want to change the company's employee-ownership structure. "If we were to find a buyer at some point for the business, would they be committed to the same social investment metrics that we put into our charter? That's the question," says Liberty.

Companies can now register as a benefit corporation in 20 US states, including Delaware (the home of US corporate law, where more than 50 percent of public companies and two-thirds of the Fortune 500 are registered), and the idea is spreading. Many more states are considering introducing the legislation, as are the governments of some other countries, including Chile and Mexico. And the passage of the legislation in Delaware has accelerated adoption, with more than 60 companies there using the new corporate form in the first three months. So far, the number of companies incorporated under the new rules is relatively small (by early 2014, there were more than 500),[54] but by laying the foundation for a revolution in the way business is done, benefit corporation legislation could go a long way toward building the impact investing sector.

Policy Measures

With the 2010 FIFA World Cup capturing the nation's imagination, few South Africans paid much attention when, that same year, the South African Treasury proposed revisions to Regulation 28, a law governing pension fund investment practices. The revisions established guidelines that paved the way for explicit analysis of environmental, social, and governance (ESG) information to be incorporated into pension fund investment decision-making processes. According to some estimates, the guidelines apply to $121 million in private pension funds and an additional $110 million in assets held in the government employee pension fund. The revised guidelines also allowed pension funds to invest in alternative assets such as private equity, a popular asset class among impact investors, and explicitly encouraged investments that also contribute to the country's development goals.[55]

Policy measures can seem remote when you're making day-to-day investment decisions. But by supporting the growth of impact investing, governments play a critical role in making life easier for you as an impact investor. In fact, the places where the most mature impact investing activity can be found are those where government policy (whether in the form of mandates, tax breaks, or guarantees) has served as a catalyst for the flow of capital. So while the revisions to Regulation 28 may not have made the headlines, they are an example of how regulatory changes can dramatically open up opportunities for investors to harness private capital for social and environmental impact.

Governments can create an enabling environment for impact investing in a number of ways. One is by introducing the benefit corporation legislation we have just discussed. Other policy measures include the following:

- **Providing carrots and sticks.** Through taxation systems, governments can provide lower corporate income taxes for high-impact businesses or lower capital gains tax for impact investments in high-impact businesses. In the United States, the New Markets Tax Credit provides tax credit incentives to investors making equity investments in certified community development entities, organizations that invest in low-income communities. Other examples include the Low Income Housing Tax Credit (for affordable housing investments) and the Community Reinvestment Act (requiring banks and other financial institutions to provide credit to the communities in which they operate, including low-income groups). The Reserve Bank of India's Priority Sector Lending requires a similar contribution.
- **Creating or funding incubators.** In the United Kingdom, the government's £10 million Social Incubator Fund is designed to provide investment funding for incubator organizations that offer intensive support to social enterprise start-ups, giving entrepreneurs the resources they need to turn early-stage ideas into successful businesses.
- **Making equity investments.** Some governments are supporting new, growing, or privatizing emerging market companies, as the United States is by making equity and equity-related investments

through the Overseas Private Investment Corporation. In May 2012, for example, OPIC pledged $87.5 million in financing for its first fund-of-funds, with a proposal to invest in 12 to 18 private equity funds investing in emerging and frontier market SMEs (small- and medium-size enterprises) that are expected to contribute economic growth, employment, and goods and services to underserved communities.[56] Governments can also use development funding to make investments that advance impact investing. For example, the United Kingdom's Department for International Development (DfID) has launched a £75 millon fund that will invest in impact investment fund managers and other intermediaries that provide capital to impact enterprises and social entrepreneurs in sub-Saharan Africa and South Asia.[57]

- **Adjusting purchasing policies and practices.** Targeted procurement policies can provide support for certain types of businesses, such as women, minority-owned businesses, or high-impact businesses that meet ratings or certification standards or whose corporate form enshrines their mission. In April 2012, for example, San Francisco passed legislation giving procurement incentives to benefit corporations in the Bay Area. Governments can also provide opportunities for social impact bonds (SIBs) or pay-for-success initiatives.

- **Financing the development of market infrastructure.** Some countries are launching banks, funds, or financial products that can improve the quality or quantity of investable deals. In the United Kingdom, Big Society Capital was established with £400m in funds in dormant bank accounts and £200m from leading banks to stimulate the creation of social finance investment intermediaries (SIFIs), which manage funds and create and raise investment for funds that provide loans or invest equity in social-sector organizations. Rather than funding social enterprises directly, the institution, under the founding leadership of Sir Ronald Cohen, Harvey McGrath, and Nick O'Donohoe, hopes to give rise to a network of specialized socially motivated lenders and investment funds that will take on that role[58]—ultimately giving government a bigger bang for its buck.

- **Raising awareness of impact investing.** National governments are beginning to take significant leadership in promoting the field as well. As part of its G8 presidency, the UK government held a one-day forum and launched the G8 Social Impact Investment Taskforce, which is advised by National Advisory Boards in each country. The Canadian government has established a new taskforce on social finance to advance alternative thinking about investing and philanthropy, with the MaRs Centre for Impact Investing as the secretariat.

Many of the most mature pockets of impact investing activity exist where government policy—whether in the form of mandates, tax breaks, or guarantees or by stimulating the growth of new corporate forms—has served as a catalyst for the flow of capital. Of course, governments can also make it harder to pursue alternative approaches to investment. One example is the 2008 reinterpretation of the Employee Retirement Income Security Act (ERISA), a US law that governs standards of conduct for pension plan fiduciaries. The reinterpretation stated that when making investment decisions, managers should assess a plan in terms of its economic returns alone, with secondary purposes considered only if "economically indistinguishable" from this primary purpose. Some have suggested this reinterpretation deterred plan managers from considering impact investments.[59] Efforts are under way to have this guidance revised so that more pension plan capital can be unlocked and put to work in the pursuit of social and environmental change.

As an impact investor, having some awareness of these developments is an important part of participating in the impact investing sphere.

Conclusion

From policy changes to measurement systems, all support tools are necessary for the long-term development of the impact investing industry. This is something GIIN's Amit Bouri argues strongly for. Realizing the full potential of impact investing, he says, requires "further strengthening the networks, information tools, and intermediaries that facilitate the flow of knowledge and capital."[60]

The nature of impact measurement and management will continue to spark debate, particularly questions such as whether general or specific assessments of social benefit are most appropriate and how impact can be attributed to individual investors. However, the good news is that an ecosystem is rapidly emerging to support impact investing, with smart thinkers and energetic activists bringing their skills and ideas to bear on propelling this industry forward and making it easier for you to engage in this form of investing.

Alongside them, new entrants to the field are expanding in number. All this gives us good reason to believe that impact investing is more than a passing fad. In the next chapter, we will look at how the field is growing globally, with increased investment activity in emerging markets as countries and regions that were once largely destinations for impact investing capital become homes to a new group of impact investors.

CHAPTER 5

A Global Movement

The 2013 Sankalp Forum in Mumbai wasn't like other social entrepreneurship conferences. For one, there was dancing. For another, it brought together the entire ecosystem for impact investing and social enterprise in India, with more than 1,000 delegates and 80 speakers. But most notably perhaps, it was the largest summit outside Europe or the United States to focus on impact investing.

The excitement surrounding the Sankalp Forum gives an indication of the dynamism at work in some of the world's emerging markets. Many people think of these markets as *destinations* for capital from impact investors based in industrialized countries. However, as patterns of global wealth shift, wealth is increasingly being amassed in Beijing, Mumbai, and São Paulo as well as Hong Kong, London, and New York. This wealth is creating a new generation of investors and philanthropists who want to see their values reflected in their investment choices and are looking for market-based mechanisms through which to contribute to human development and environmental sustainability in their countries. As a result, emerging markets are increasingly *sources* of capital—sources that so far remain relatively untapped but are sure to become more important over time.

A rich universe of entrepreneurs and investment opportunities is emerging throughout the developing world. In the process, national borders are breaking down. Take James Chen, who makes his impact investments largely through direct investments and start-up ventures. Chen is from an entrepreneurial Chinese family whose business has been based in Nigeria for the past 50 years. He was in Switzerland when he was first drawn to this form of investing after hearing the term *blended value* at a conference there. One of his investments is in Adlens, a British company he also cofounded, with offices in Boston, Tokyo, and Hong Kong. The company makes affordable plastic eyeglasses with lenses that can be adjusted to the correct focus by turning a knob. "It's still burning cash," says Chen, "but we're close to a breakthrough, and it's been a fascinating journey." In the developing world, Adlens has focused on Rwanda, funding hundreds of health centers and the training of staff so that no one is more than five kilometers away from an eye exam. "If we are successful, Rwandans within the next three to five years will have better vision than people in any other country in the world," he says, adding that he has been invited to pilot the same initiative in Haiti by the country's prime minister. Chen has also been very active as an angel investor in a cardiovascular clinic in Shanghai, which he hopes will demonstrate a new model of patient-centered care in China.

Chen's investment activities span continents and countries. He is just one example of how pioneering impact investors are thinking and acting globally. Perhaps you are among them, and you're reading this book from Mexico City, New Delhi, Buenos Aires, or Lagos. Or maybe you're sitting in London, Munich, San Francisco, or New York but would like to gain a better sense of the local investment landscape in the places where you might invest. Wherever you are, as an impact investor, you are not alone. This is an increasingly global market. And the movement of capital is not one way—impact investment funds flow in many directions and across many borders, both north and south.

Some markets are just starting out on their impact investing journey. In the Middle East, for example, impact investing is a nascent industry, while in India, an increasingly sophisticated community of impact investors is emerging. Each market is distinct and diverse. Yet despite the variances in impact investing across emerging markets, they generally share a few notable challenges and unique opportunities that distinguish them from regions such as Europe and North America. These include:

- **Significant human development needs.** A wide range of countries fall under the umbrella term *emerging markets*, and the availability of essential human services such as health care, education, and (increasingly) elderly care services varies significantly. What all these countries have in common, however, is that large numbers of their citizens lack access to services that are of adequate quality—even in countries such as India and Brazil, which are home to increasing wealth. In East Asia, where human development levels are the highest outside Europe and North America, most countries are grappling with the prospect of rapidly aging populations and insufficient elderly care services.

- **Weak domestic credit and equity markets, particularly for SMEs.** The reach and sophistication of the financial sector vary across countries and regions, but gaps in the supply of debt and equity finance exist in many places. These gaps are particularly pronounced for small- and medium-size enterprises (SMEs). With between 10 and 250 employees, these enterprises are not typically able to access the services of microfinance institutions or major banks. We do not believe that all SME finance constitutes impact investing (since much of it lacks the intent to create positive impact as described in chapter 1), but limited access to capital combined with high human development needs often creates impact investing opportunities.

- **The prominence of family businesses.** Another factor many emerging markets have in common is the prominence of family businesses in the private sector. In Asia in particular, family businesses are engines of growth. In most Asian countries, family-controlled businesses make up more than 60 percent of listed companies with market capitalizations higher than $50 million, according to the CFA Institute.[61] The profile of a typical impact investor in the United States (someone who generated meaningful levels of wealth when his or her company was bought or sold) is much less common in other regions. Family businesses, on the other hand, often have a significant ongoing social and environmental footprint and have opportunities to use that footprint to make a positive impact on communities or the environment. Many family businesses appear willing to do that, but they are not a constituency that is traditionally targeted by the impact investing community. While some family businesses participate in impact investing (particularly in India, for example), there is potential to harness some of the resources of this community of businesses as impact investing markets mature around the world. If you are part of one of these family businesses, this book should provide you with what you need to get started.

- **A relatively weak formal philanthropic sector.** While in places such as the United States, philanthropy has been a driving force behind the adoption of impact investing, in many emerging markets the philanthropic sector is in a relatively nascent state. In Latin America, state and religious institutions have long shouldered the burden of providing social services. In East and Southeast Asia, giving is often driven by family values and religion. Few large institutions have been established, and those that do exist have done little to experiment with strategic or innovative philanthropy. The relative scarcity of philanthropic funding in these regions creates a gap in funding for early-stage, high-risk ventures and makes it hard to finance the building of the networks, institutions, and measurement systems needed to support the growth of impact investing. Fortunately, the philanthropic sector is poised to grow rapidly across most regions, and global philanthropies such as the Rockefeller Foundation are stepping in to provide the initial start-up capital for the field of impact investing.

- **Lack of familiarity with impact investing.** In many emerging markets, *impact investing* is an unfamiliar term. In these places, while impact investing–type activity may be taking place, it has not yet been defined as such. In countries with very low levels of per capita income, or very high rates of unemployment, the line between "impact investing" and "private-sector development" may be fuzzy. We and others are working to spread knowledge and understanding of impact investing in markets where opportunity exists but is unrealized. In 2012 and 2013 the Rockefeller Foundation partnered with other leaders in the field to organize major events in São Paulo, Bangalore, Hong Kong, and Cape Town that helped raise awareness and build collective action in places where we believe impact investing has significant potential but is relatively nascent.
- **Interest in impact investing from development organizations.** While we have so far emphasized the challenges, one positive factor differentiating developing countries is the fact that many multilateral institutions and development banks—including the Inter-American Development Bank, the World Bank's International Finance Corporation (IFC), and the United States' Overseas Private Investment Corporation (OPIC)—are becoming interested in impact investing. They see it as a way of harnessing private-sector dollars to advance their development agendas. And with large amounts of funding at their disposal, these organizations could play a critical role in advancing the adoption of impact investing.

Markets are evolving at different speeds and with varying degrees of sophistication. But we believe that investors in emerging economies will play a critical role in helping the impact investing sector grow and realize its potential to change people's lives. If you are from one of these countries, you may have recognized this.

The link between investors and the ultimate destinations of their funds is even stronger in emerging markets than elsewhere, since local investors are typically closer to the problems their countries face. As an investor in an emerging market, you may better understand the challenges smallholder farmers confront as they try to access more resilient seed stocks, for example, and how this might be overcome through an impact investment. You may understand how and why slum-dwellers need to upgrade or move into new homes, and how impact investing might provide the funds needed to construct them and the micro-loans that will make them a possibility for poor communities.

It is critical to highlight the potential for leadership of investors in the emerging markets, because they are drivers of innovation and owners of an increasing share of the world's capital. We also believe that their full participation helps protect impact investing from exposure to some of the problematic dynamics that have plagued traditional aid and development finance. And we believe that socially focused business models and innovative forms of financing have the potential not only to materialize in emerging markets, but also to inspire and inform investors in mature economies. In this chapter, we'll give you a taste of how impact investing is developing in emerging markets.

South Asia

In India in particular, the past 15 years have taken impact investing to a more mature stage than in many other markets. Along the way, a number of socioeconomic and political factors have helped create conditions that favor (and sometimes hinder) the use of market-based approaches to problems such as pollution, poverty, and lack of access to education or health care.

Here, impact investing has been fueled by a dynamic cohort of social enterprises and entrepreneurs, and by support from the public and private sectors. In 2009 a report conducted by Monitor Group (now part of Deloitte Consulting) found that in India, new market-based enterprises were in many cases providing services to the poorest in society more effectively than government or nonprofits. Among other findings, the report found that these enterprises were providing clean drinking water at one-fourth the cost of the least expensive alternative; that for about three dollars a month, private schools in urban slums were outperforming top government education institutions; and that safe, doctor-attended births could be conducted for less than one-fourth the price charged in traditional private hospitals.[62]

South Asia's robust microfinance industries (particularly in India and Bangladesh) have laid the groundwork for private-sector engagement in social impact and, as a result, for the emergence of infrastructure and measurement systems. Policy is also a strong force in India, where the government has long encouraged private-sector participation in development. The Reserve Bank of India required all banks with operations in India to direct a fixed percentage of lending to underserved, or "priority," sectors, including agriculture, small enterprise, retail trade, education, and housing finance. A number of banks fill this requirement by lending money to microfinance institutions, which in turn lend funds to the unbanked. More recently, the Indian government's National Innovation Council announced the formation of the India Inclusive Innovation Fund as a means of helping create an ecosystem of entrepreneurship and venture capital targeted at innovative solutions to poverty, with capital to come from government, state-run companies, banks, and private investors.

While microfinance in India has helped pave the way for a broader impact investing industry in a number of respects, controversies surrounding microfinance have dampened enthusiasm for the private sector's role in development. Perhaps most famously, in the Indian state of Andhra Pradesh, high interest rates, overindebtedness among borrowers who had loans with multiple institutions, and allegations of corruption led to a government crackdown on microcredit and to public debate over the legitimacy of high profit margins earned by companies serving poor people. Even so, such controversies have provided lessons from which to build and, while painful, have also prompted necessary and sophisticated discussions about consumer protection, commercialization, and regulation.

When it comes to promoting private-sector approaches to social impact, India has several advantages. First, the country has many tech-savvy young people able to plug into the networks, financing, and support needed to help put an idea into action. Second, India has several successful business models that tap into an extremely large population of low-income consumers, whether smallholder farmers or women looking for affordable maternity care.

Meanwhile, the country has both a strong nonprofit and civil-society sector and major corporate-sector players that have traditionally made commitments to social issues. While these corporate commitments are largely CSR initiatives, they follow principles and practices similar to those of impact investments. Hindustan Unilever's Shakti program, for instance, trains women in rural India to distribute its products, expanding both their incomes and the company's sales, while the Tata Group has developed a range of products (from affordable housing to a water purifier) targeted at low-income groups.

The combination of these factors has helped foster a vibrant social enterprise sector, providing a rich seam of opportunities for impact investors. The Monitor Group study surveyed more than 300 market-based initiatives in India involving companies, nonprofits, and state authorities, describing India as "a pacesetter among emerging markets" in social entrepreneurship.[63]

On the demand side, too, the impact investment community is a relatively well-developed sector in India. The Unitus family of enterprises (which brings together an equity fund, a seed fund, an early-stage venture investment firm, a financial and capital advisory firm, and an incubator to "reduce global poverty through economic self-empowerment") is largely concentrated in India.

Indian fund manager Aavishkaar has been investing in early-stage enterprises since 2001, and has built up a track record of investments in high-impact scalable enterprises in sectors such as agriculture and dairy, education, energy, handicrafts, health, water and sanitation, technology for development, and financial inclusion.

Aavishkaar's venture capital activities have grown rapidly since then, and its fourth fund, the Aavishkaar II, achieved its final close at $94 million, with lead investments from both public- and private-sector organizations, including the World Bank's International Finance Corporation, the CDC (the United Kingdom's development finance institution), and Cisco, the US computer networking company. Over the past decade, with its sister company, Intellecap, Aavishkaar has focused on building the ecosystem needed to address the "pioneer gap" in early-stage investing though initiatives that include the Sankalp Forum, angel networks such as Intellecap (the only dedicated impact angel network in India) and I3N, and IntelleGrow, a debt-financing firm focused on small businesses.

Meanwhile, a set of angel investors is emerging in India. Mainstream angel networks such as the Indian Angel Network (which was launched in 2006 and has become one of the leading investors in start-ups and early-stage ventures) have recently begun to dip a toe into impact investing. Indian Angel Network, whose primary focus is commercial returns, aims to make investments of up to $1 million and exit in between three and five years via a sale, an IPO, or a merger or acquisition. Investments in its portfolio range from IndiaCollegeSearch (an online platform that helps students looking for a college differentiate among different institutions and apply instantly) to nithya (an edgy, high-end designer brand that aims to reposition Sri Lanka's ancient handloom craft[64]). Meanwhile, India's first angel network dedicated specifically to impact investing, the Intellecap Impact Investor Network, was launched in 2011 and often co-invests with investors from around the world, such as members of United States–based angel network Toniic.

While India is at the center of the activity in the region, impact enterprises and market-based models of addressing social and environmental challenges are emerging in countries such as Bangladesh, Pakistan, and Sri Lanka. Bangladesh, for example, is considered the birthplace of modern microfinance because of the pioneering role of Bangladeshi institutions such as Grameen Bank and BRAC. More recently, some of the funds that have historically focused on India, including Aavishkaar, are raising money to invest in countries such as Bangladesh and Sri Lanka.

At the same time, innovative social enterprises are cropping up across South Asia. Take the Saiban project in Pakistan, for example, where Tasneem Siddiqui, a social entrepreneur, is developing a residential community of simple, compact row houses that has an inventive cross-subsidization system for financing, marketing, and selling the homes—about 75 percent of the plots are sold on a nonprofit basis to families earning less than four dollars a day. To make sure that the low-cost homes go to those that need them, potential buyers must live on the site during construction, a rule that deters speculators who simply want to flip the properties for profit.[65] Despite this progress, views on the nature of South Asia's market diverge. Some observers see a lack of adequate funding for the early-stage companies developing new business models to serve or employ people at the "Bottom of the Pyramid"—something the Monitor Group described as a "pioneer gap."[66] A pioneer gap threatens the entire industry by limiting the pipeline of companies that grow to accommodate larger or more commercial forms of capital.

Still, others believe that there is an adequate supply of viable companies and that the problem lies in the available supply of appropriate capital. "India has lately seen the emergence of numerous impact funds, yet successful Indian entrepreneurs continue to remain starved of capital," says Vineet Rai, Aavishkaar's founder. "What we need in India today is capital that is hardworking, risk-taking and truly patient in large quantity."

Both perspectives have their merits. Nevertheless, few dispute the fact that, with India leading the charge, the region's impact investing ecosystem has moved far ahead of those found in other emerging markets and is ripe with opportunities.

East and Southeast Asia

Soaring skyscrapers and luxury goods stores paint a picture of a region that has experienced extremely rapid growth. But behind the glitz is the reality that many East and Southeast Asians still live in abject poverty and the region faces enormous environmental challenges. Yet with $10 trillion sitting in the accounts of high-net-worth individuals in the region, tremendous opportunity exists to unlock private capital and apply it to some of the region's social and environmental challenges.[67]

Despite its potential, however, little leadership on impact investing has emerged in the region compared with other parts of the world, and significant structural weaknesses mean plenty of work remains to be done before impact investment can take hold. Lack of a formal philanthropic sector is one problem. Religions such as Buddhism in Thailand or Catholicism in the Philippines, combined with the strength of Asia's family ties, have given charitable and community efforts deep roots in the region. But few large foundations exist, and tax incentives to promote more formal philanthropy are rare. As in many emerging markets, this leaves the industry without what in Europe and the United States have proved to be key local players in promoting impact investing through field-building work and grant funding for early-stage social enterprises.

Still, hubs of activity can be found, particularly in Hong Kong and Singapore, along with emerging communities of practice in countries such as Thailand and Indonesia. Pioneering individuals and institutions are contributing to the formation of a regional ecosystem. And across the continent, the Asian Development Bank, the region's development finance institution, is looking at impact investing as a means of furthering its agenda.

In China, impact investing is still in its infancy. However, some see it and social enterprise as more acceptable to the Chinese authorities and others than grant making to nonprofit organizations. In a reversal of the order in which things have developed in the United States and Europe, impact investments in China, some believe, could be a bridge to philanthropy and to the growth of the civil-society sector.

Impact investing is being explored by some of those leading the development of the country's nascent philanthropic sector. One example is You Cheng (the You Change Foundation), which is raising a renminbi impact investing fund. Meanwhile, Yu Venture Philanthropy (launched by Venture Avenue, a philanthropic consulting firm founded by former Boston Consulting Group executive Robin Zhang) has also played a role. In March 2012 it joined forces with the Xinhu Group and the Amity Foundation to create the ¥10 million Yu Venture Philanthropy Fund.

Meanwhile, a few pioneering investment firms are expanding the number of opportunities open to impact investors in the region. These include Tsing Capital, whose portfolio includes clean energy, sustainable agriculture, and sustainable transport companies; and Yimei Capital, a ¥50 million fund, with funding from both government and individuals. China Impact Fund (CIF) is an impact venture fund managed by Dao Ventures, a China-focused impact investment firm. CIF is the first impact fund in China to specialize in financing and accelerating the growth of SMEs providing environmentally friendly products and services and of start-up companies promoting sustainable land use, clean energy, and water access in poor communities.

James Chen believes the time is ripe for impact investing in China. "One of the things I love is that there are a lot of energetic young people in China who see the issues and want to work on solutions," he says. "They are often hampered by lack of support from the government, which is why this is a promising avenue."

A leader in the region is Singapore, which is positioning itself as a gateway to Southeast Asia for everything from financial services to foreign investors, tourism, and the arts. With a multilingual workforce, favorable tax regime, trusted legal system, well-developed financial services sector, and robust intellectual property protection, the island state is well placed to help lead innovations in social financing.

Singapore is also home to a growing number of impact investing funds and intermediaries, including Impact Investment Exchange Asia (IIX). IIX works to build awareness of impact investing in South and Southeast Asia and operates both public and private exchanges that enable companies and funds to raise capital based on their social, environmental, and financial performance. IIX's Impact Exchange, which trades out of Mauritius, will provide listing and admission procedures, market rules, and disclosure requirements that give investors transparency into social enterprises.

By contrast, in Hong Kong, a small but pioneering cadre of local investors and entrepreneurs is largely behind the creation of the impact ecosystem. Asia Community Ventures, which is home to investors who care about both domestic and international challenges, serves as a hub for activity in the territory. Boutique impact investment firms are being established in Hong Kong, too. Avantage Ventures, a social investment company with offices also in Beijing, was created to fill what the firm calls the "missing middle" financing gap for enterprises focused on solving social and environmental challenges and seeking investments of between $500,000 and $3 million.[68]

Hong Kong is also home to one of the early leaders in impact investing, Annie Chen, who invests through her family office, RS Group. Motivated by her belief in the importance of sustainable development and her conviction that social entrepreneurs can deliver that change, Chen is moving her entire portfolio to investments that can create sustainable impact. This portfolio approach is still a work in progress and provides an interesting model for others to explore and follow.

While Singapore and Hong Kong are centers of activity, interest in harnessing private-sector methods and capital to address social and environmental challenges is emerging across Southeast Asia. Events such as the annual Social Enterprise Summit in Hong Kong and the recent Impact Forum in Singapore drew hundreds of participants from around the region.

Excitement in these kinds of new business models is particularly intense among young executives. For example, since 2007, a version of the annual Global Social Venture Competition (an initiative of the Haas School of Business at University of California, Berkeley, that identifies and helps launch promising social enterprises) has been running in Thailand, organized by the Thammasat Business School. The competition attracts teams from Brunei, Cambodia, Indonesia, Laos, Malaysia, Myanmar, Singapore, Oceania, the Philippines, Thailand, and Vietnam.

Despite such pockets of enthusiasm, however, East and Southeast Asia still have some way to go in developing a sustainable impact investing sector. In the 2013 GIIN–J.P. Morgan survey, 42 percent of respondents answered "none" or "few" when asked about the number of East and Southeast Asian investment opportunities considered in 2012 that passed initial impact and financial screens.[69]

For those who'd like to be leaders in seeding the impact investing industry in one or more countries in Southeast Asia, this presents an opportunity: despite a growing number of new intermediaries and impact funds, more early-stage funding (particularly from philanthropists) is needed to support these enterprises. Philo Alto, cofounder of Asia Community Ventures in Hong Kong, identifies "a lack of risk-appropriate philanthropic funding for the vast majority of social businesses in Asia that are either too young or too small in scale to be considered 'impact investment ready.'" He argues that "more support by philanthropic funders and venture philanthropy intermediaries is needed."[70]

If such support can be found, and if a robust ecosystem for impact investing evolves, the potential is enormous. Avantage Ventures estimates that by 2020, the amount of investment needs for social enterprises in six sectors (affordable housing, water and sanitation, rural energy, rural and elderly health care, primary education, and agribusiness) will total between $44 billion and $74 billion and that, if invested, those funds could unlock a market demand of between $52 billion and $158 billion.[71]

Latin America

With prominent impact investing funds emerging (such as IGNIA, the Mexico-based impact investing venture capital fund, and Brazil-based Vox Capital), there is evidence of growing interest in impact investing in the region. So far the market remains fragmented and makes up just a tiny proportion of the region's capital markets activity. And the philanthropic sector has not played a catalytic role in developing market-based approaches to social and environmental challenges. Yet underlying social and economic factors make Latin American a promising region for the growth of impact investing.

As in South Asia, the microfinance industry has paved the way for market-based approaches to be applied to social problems. In many Latin American countries, microfinance is a robust sector, with long-established institutions making small loans to small entrepreneurs running businesses that provide low-income communities with everything from purified water and education kits to affordable home improvement materials and building services—enterprises that could also be targets for impact investment funds.

Meanwhile, with a feeling among the younger generation of wealthy individuals and businesspeople that "business as usual" cannot meet the region's challenges, the appetite for alternative approaches to human development and environmental sustainability is growing. Evidence for this can be found in the strong support for the Social Investment Task Force initiated in Brazil in 2013, and for the country's first impact investing conference scheduled to take place in 2014.

Areas of energy and dynamism are emerging throughout the region. A striking example is the Empresa B movement in Argentina, Chile, and Colombia, which includes TriCiclos and a number of other pioneering enterprises. (Empresa B companies are the Latin American counterparts to B Corporation enterprises found in the United States, discussed in the previous chapter.)

Individuals and philanthropists also are promoting impact investment in Latin America. In Brazil, this includes the family offices of the founders of Natura Cosmetics (Luiz Seabra, Guilherme Leal, and Pedro Passos), who are particularly interested in housing and property rights, health, recycling, education, forestry, and renewable energy. Around the region, the Fundación Avina actively supports inclusive business strategies such as micro- and small enterprises, corporate social responsibility, green businesses, and cooperative movements.

One challenge is the current disparity between the number of impact investing activities in wealthier areas and that in poorer parts of the region. While a substantial amount of investment is flowing into SMEs in cities and wealthier parts, much less is reaching rural areas and poorer regions. Another challenge is that the infrastructure required to support impact investing (such as the adoption of information and measurement systems) remains nascent at best. And even when capital can be mobilized, there is a need for more viable enterprises with the access to skills, networks, and markets needed to use that capital productively.

Challenges aside, regional and international institutions are showing strong support for impact investing. In Latin America and the Caribbean, the Inter-American Development Bank (IDB) is promoting impact investing as a development tool by forming partnerships with institutional investors, foundations, companies, and high-net-worth individuals. As well as providing technical assistance for these projects, the IDB is working with impact investors to cofinance projects though equity investments, syndicated loans, and partial credit guarantees. Some of these cofinancing projects engage governments. For example, the Inter-American Investment Corporation (part of the IDB) established China-IIC SME Equity Investment Trust Fund with the support of the People's Republic of China, to boost equity investments in Latin America and the Caribbean. The fund is designed to provide financing for SMEs through equity and quasi-equity instruments.

International nonprofits are also stepping in to support impact enterprises. In Chile, San Francisco–based NESsT (which provides financing, training, mentoring, and market access for social enterprises in emerging markets) has launched a program to support social enterprises with workshops on everything from enterprise development and product quality improvement to sales and marketing techniques. And with a strong presence in Latin America, Washington, DC-based TechnoServe provides business advice, access to markets, and capital to entrepreneurs, particularly in the food and agriculture sectors.

Some policy and regulatory frameworks are also helping to create a more robust impact investing ecosystem. In Colombia, for example, Pioneros de la Innovación Social, a collaboration between the government, the IDB, and several of Colombia's biggest companies, is providing seed funding and mentoring to impact-oriented start-ups. Several countries are also looking at the possibility of introducing benefit corporation legislation.[72]

These kinds of developments are encouraging and should provide opportunities for you if your emphasis is on Latin America. For although much still needs to be done to build the region's impact investing ecosystem and infrastructure, Latin American countries are poised to harness this investment approach as a means of addressing some of their biggest challenges.

Africa

Perhaps nowhere can impact investing have a greater role than in Africa. Although wealthy investors are not as numerous there as in other parts of the world, the continent is home to great dynamism and tremendous contradictions. While it has been invoked in recent years as a "rising continent" and one of the few regions to return double-digit growth rates, it is also home to some of the highest rates of poverty, hunger, and inequality in the world. The opportunities, and challenges, of Africa make it a compelling location for business models that seek to generate positive impact as well as profit.

Many forces at work in Africa could power the emergence of impact enterprises on the continent. Africa is on the brink of a "youth bulge"—by 2050 its youth population is set to double to 400 million, more than that of South Asia, providing a promising source of human capital.[73] What's more, the mobile revolution and growth of the ICT sector has done much to enable new business models for impact enterprises. Real-time, text-based data on commodities markets now empower smallholder farmers. Mobile money transfer services such as Kenya's M-Pesa provide basic financial services to millions of unbanked citizens and microentrepreneurs. At the same time, falling prices for renewable energy infrastructure are helping fuel a range of enterprise models designed to address energy poverty and reduce carbon emissions. Some of Africa's most promising enterprise models are entirely homegrown, while others have been adapted from models that have proved successful in other regions, especially India.

There is also a diverse range of capital sources on the continent that can be channeled toward impact investing, from microfunding to institutional investment. Remittances from the African diaspora often help small businesses get off the ground, and these funds could be used more strategically and systematically. Meanwhile, institutional investors such as pension funds and insurance companies are waiting in the wings as pockets of capital accumulate in countries such as South Africa and Nigeria—South Africa alone has $250 billion in pension fund assets.[74]

While there are many positive trends at work, the scale of the challenges cannot be underestimated. One of the most pressing is the urbanization of the continent—which is more rapid than anywhere else in the world. Massive numbers of people flocking to the continent's cities are straining infrastructure, food, and resources. Unplanned slum expansion continues at an alarming pace, leaving millions of citizens without access to adequate housing, clean water, or sanitation and creating traffic chaos and pollution. Without the right policies and infrastructure investments, economic inequities and environmental degradation will only increase.

In response to these challenges, impact enterprises are emerging across the region, often employing innovative business models. For many impact investors, the models created in India should prove valuable. Already working in sub-Saharan African countries are impact investors focusing on agriculture and supporting smallholder farmers in improving both their incomes and the environmental sustainability of their operations. In Tanzania, for instance, Mtanga Farms helps improve livelihoods for low-income families in rural areas by improving farmers' access to agricultural inputs, technology, and markets. In Kenya, Juhudi Kilimo provides asset-linked financing to livestock and poultry farmers. Because the loans are based on an income-generating asset, it can offer lower interest rates than would be possible with general loans and it can accommodate staggered or longer repayment periods that are linked to clients' sales and revenue.

These kinds of enterprises have long been a focus of impact investors in Europe and the United States. In the 2013 GIIN–J.P. Morgan survey of investors, most of whom were based in North America and Europe, the largest group (34 percent) of respondents reported a focus on investing in sub-Saharan Africa.[75] In recent years, a number of dedicated impact investing funds have started to operate in Africa. Using both local and international funding sources, they are providing new supplies of capital to the continent's dynamic ecosystem of social enterprises. And with growing pools of capital in Nigeria and South Africa, there is potential to direct even larger-size funds into the continent's impact enterprises.

To realize this potential, however, some of the barriers to the expansion of impact investing on the continent need to be addressed. First, impact investing is not yet a commonly understood concept in Africa, and more than perhaps in any other region, the term can easily be conflated with private-sector development generally. In Francophone Africa, cooperatives are a common form of enterprise organization, and few formal means of financing these collective organizations with third-party capital have yet been developed. More work also needs to be done to increase the supply of viable investment opportunities. The GIIN–J.P. Morgan survey found a weak pipeline of opportunities for impact investors. When asked about the number of investment opportunities considered in 2012 in different regions that passed an initial impact and financial screen, 77 percent of respondents said "none" or "few" in the Middle East and Africa.[76]

Some worry that in Africa not enough "patient" (long-term) capital is available, while concerns remain over whether investments will prove economically viable and politically stable. Others question whether sufficient human capital exists and whether there are sufficient numbers of investment-ready enterprises and entrepreneurs. Unfortunately, there is little evidence that investors are ready to provide money and technical assistance for early-stage investments. Research by the Acumen Fund and Monitor Group (now Deloitte) has documented the long and slow path to profitability of many impact enterprises in Africa as well as other regions, while finding that only six of the 84 funds investing in those regions offered early-stage capital.[77]

Nevertheless, pioneering investors and entrepreneurs are emerging, paving the way for others to follow. In April 2013, the Rockefeller Foundation and the Nigeria-based Tony Elumelu Foundation announced the launch of the Impact Economy Innovations Fund (IEIF), which is designed to fund projects that harness market-based solutions, foster entrepreneurial ecosystems, and promote impact investing industry infrastructure in Africa.

There are also regional and international actors willing to roll up their sleeves to combine investment dollars with technical assistance. In Rwanda, for example, the UK-based Gatsby Trust arranged for the purchase of an underperforming tea factory and secured a management contract from neighboring Kenya Tea Development Agency, which had a strong track record in working with smallholder tea farmers. Gatsby plans to sell the factory to 25,000 smallholder farmers over the next seven years, and estimates that the combination of higher production and ownership participation will increase their earnings by 1,000 percent. In the meantime, however, Gatsby is committing significant resources to develop human capital, value-added production strategies, managerial capacity, and governance structures among the farmers.

In Mozambique, work is under way to explore how a development impact bond might provide a solution to arresting the spread of malaria through the distribution of mosquito nets. The Mozambican government has joined forces with Dalberg, the development consultancy; Nando's, a South Africa–based restaurant chain; and Anglo American, the mining group, to develop a plan to issue a $25 or $30 million bond in early 2014. In a pay-for-success model, returns would come from mining companies working in Mozambique in the form of the savings they make as a result of the increased productivity and improved health of their workers.[78]

In some countries, governments are introducing legislative measures to encourage the development of this approach to investing, not only removing barriers to impact investing but actively encouraging it. In Ghana, for example, venture capital funds and their portfolio companies enjoy a range of tax benefits.[79] In South Africa, Regulation 28 is designed to "ensure that the savings South Africans contribute toward their retirement is invested in a prudent manner that not only protects the retirement fund member, but is channeled in ways that achieve economic development and growth."[80]

As with emerging markets in general, it is hard to generalize when assessing progress on impact investing in Africa. In South Africa, large pools of wealth, a strong culture of corporate responsibility, and a sophisticated financial sector have helped the impact investing market reach a more mature stage of development than in many places. Elsewhere, much work needs to be done to lay the foundations for impact investing and to persuade both governments and investors that impact investing is a means of promoting sustainable growth in Africa while also offering the possibility of attractive financial returns.

Conclusion

In emerging markets, the number and diversity of new entrants to the impact investing field is increasing rapidly—from Brazil and South Africa to China and Thailand. While each region presents unique challenges and opportunities, collectively they are ensuring that impact investing is a truly global industry, with each taking its place among an increasingly international community of leaders, innovators, and practitioners. So, if your investment strategies take you to any of these regions, you are likely to find allies and mentors. Moreover, because they can draw upon global best practices and tools, newer entrants are well positioned to ramp up more quickly than their predecessors. In turn, they are likely to reshape the way things are done in more mature markets. Brazil-based Vox Capital, for example, visited Indian veteran Aavishkaar when it was first forming and adapted and built on many of its innovations. Now Vox is helping lead the way in experimental fund structures and is pushing the envelope on impact measurement and management. More than a decade earlier, Michele Giddens took her eight years of experience at Shorebank Corporation, one of the original US-based Community Development Finance Institutions, and used it to cofound Bridges Ventures in the United Kingdom.

The activities of Vox, Aavishkaar, ShoreBank, and Bridges offer examples for others to follow. And as the leadership of the impact investing industry becomes truly global, mutual learning will only increase, allowing everyone to benefit. Having looked at how the global impact investing community is evolving, we will now move on to offer some guidance on how you, as an investor keen to embark on or expand an impact investing strategy, can get started or work on expanding your portfolio.

CHAPTER 6

Getting Started

For many years, successful Brussels-based entrepreneur François de Borchgrave somehow found the time to combine his business activities with volunteering for nonprofit organizations and running the venture philanthropy organization he founded in 2002: Toolbox, which provides management services to nonprofits. De Borchgrave had held positions at large tech-sector companies, founded an Internet start-up, and spent ten years as a private equity investor. He loved working in support of causes that were important to him. He also loved the private equity process. But he was finding it hard to get excited about the companies in which he was investing.

So in 2009, when he first learned about impact investing, de Borchgrave saw an opportunity to continue doing the work he enjoyed while also contributing to social and environmental change. He began by defining his goals clearly, and decided he would focus on investing in health, education, and the environment in Europe and parts of the developing world. He wanted to find opportunities that would ultimately generate a competitive rate of financial return, but to which he could also apply his skills.

De Borchgrave decided to move all his investable assets into impact investments. He also went one step further and founded a specialist investment firm, Kois Invest, to help others do the same. Despite having a set of relevant skills and experiences, he wanted support as he embarked on this new path and looked around for a community of like-minded investors. At a conference, he came across a representative from Toniic, an international network of angel investors founded in 2010, and joined as one of its first Europe-based members. Being part of Toniic, he explains, has brought him into contact with other impact investors and allows him to tap into deals, share resources, and benefit from the collective wisdom of a group of informed individuals.

For de Borchgrave, impact investing allows him to combine his passions. "It's a way to invest capital in a meaningful way that's aligned to my values and the impact I want to have on the world," he says. "I can't think of anything else I would rather be doing." However, as when starting any new activity, he needed to think carefully about his goals and strategies and to seek out (as he did by joining Toniic) networks that could help him start to build knowledge and understanding of the sector.

So far, we have discussed what impact investing is, who is pursuing such investments, what support systems are needed to promote its growth, where impact investing has been able to take root, and why we believe impact investing is emerging as a powerful force in the twenty-first century.

One question remains—and we hope it's a question the preceding chapters have led you to ask: *How do I get started?* Or for folks who have already dipped their toes into the impact investing waters: *How do I become a more sophisticated impact investor?* Whichever your question, this chapter will provide some practical guidance on taking your first or next steps into the world of impact investing. Later in the chapter, we'll go into some of the actions and considerations that are specific to different types of investors.

Five Questions to Get You Started

No two impact investors are exactly the same, and impact invest-ments are diverse across many dimensions—including target impact, financial return expectations, geography, and level of investor engagement. This is part of what makes the sector so exciting and energizing. But equally, it can make it hard to figure out where to begin, particularly for new impact investors; there is no template to apply or simple form to fill out. Soul searching can be time consuming, and understanding the ecosystem of the actors involved is challenging. While finding the time is one thing that investors often have little of, some careful upfront thinking will go a long way toward helping you realize your goals. And that means posing a set of questions to yourself. Here are the ones we believe are most important:

How general or specific are your impact goals? If you have specific (rather than general) goals, what are they?

Here you should think about whether your goal is to "do good" generally, in whatever ways possible (with minimum disruption to your existing asset allocation or management strategie) or to advance specific social or environmental agendas (such as promoting local and sustainable food systems or expanding access to health care among disadvantaged communities).

Perhaps you aren't drawn to a specific issue so much as a general goal or guiding principle. That's okay. Your goal can be as general as "bringing market-based solutions to social problems" or "maximizing the overall positive environmental and social impact of your investments," which would give you more flexibility in your strategy. You could invest via the growing number of dedicated impact investing funds that have broad mandates, or you could assemble a portfolio of diverse individual investments. If you are relatively agnostic about the type of impact you would like to have, you have more latitude to focus on the other questions at hand.

Maybe you have particular goals in mind or specific values that you want to embed in your investments. Your purpose might be to advance environmental agendas such as promoting biodiversity, reducing dependence on fossil fuels, or conserving tropical forests. Or you might have social goals. If so, what are they? They might be expanding access to health care among disadvantaged communities. You might want to focus on girls' education or prison recidivism.

Whichever direction you want to take, it's important to drill deeper into how you envision your investment contributing to that change. This will inform you as you seek out direct investments or choose funds to invest in, and as you search for advisers who are best positioned to help you.

Let's say, for example, that you care deeply about the environment and want to use impact investing as a means of shifting your investments away from unsustainable assets (such as companies producing fossil fuels) and instead support clean energy, conservation, or energy efficiency investments. In this case, options span a wide range from large and commercial investments such as the Climate Solutions Fund, managed by multibillion-dollar asset manager Generation Investment Management, to very small funds such as EKO Asset Management Partners, a New York–based specialist investment firm that focuses on climate change, sustainable fisheries, and green infrastructure (such as natural solutions to reduce storm water runoff, enhance coastal resilience, restore and protect watershed ecosystems, and improve water quality and availability). You might also target individual companies such as Ethical Electric, a US renewable energy provider.

Alternatively, perhaps you are concerned about nutrition and local agriculture. You might think about investing in RSF Social Finance's Local Initiatives Fund, which invests in companies such as Bright Farms, which builds and operates hydroponic greenhouse farms at or near supermarkets. If you care about food security in developing countries, you might consider investing through an organization such as Root Capital, which provides loans and technical assistance to cooperatives and other farmer organizations in Africa and Latin America. If you want to pursue an even more specific goal, you might find direct investments in companies more appealing than investments through funds or other intermediaries.

The good news is that the rapidly growing universe of opportunity can accommodate impact investors of all types, and a diverse set of approaches is already at work. But articulating what you want to achieve is the first step toward achieving success on the path toward impact investing.

Where do you want to make an impact?

Another consideration is which, if any, geographic areas you want to reach with your investments. Again, this could be broad: you might want to address global inequality, for example, or invest in opportunities that improve the lives of people in developing countries. Or you may be more locally motivated: if you feel a strong connection to a particular community (maybe the place where you live or were raised, though it doesn't have to be so personal), you might want to use your funding as a means of supporting locally based solutions to the challenges facing that community. While impact investing is often associated with global investments that support entrepreneurs in developing countries, local investing is a frequent point of entry for many impact investors, both individual and institutional. A plethora of social and environmental issues confronts almost all communities, creating an important role for impact investing capital in most parts of the world.

So, whose lives do you most want to improve with your investments? Poor people in developing countries? People in your home country? People in your local community? Determining the nature of the positive human impact you want to make, and where you want to make it, will help you to work backward so as to find the right path forward.

What kinds of financial returns are you seeking?

The financial returns promised by impact investment funds range from concessionary to highly competitive, so recognizing on which end of the spectrum you sit is an important part of the process when identifying investments that will fit your objectives.

While impact investments by definition must generate both social and environmental financial returns, some investors are willing to take lower-than-market returns if it means achieving a greater impact with their investment. Other investors, by contrast, prioritize financial return over the amount of social impact created. If you are a private individual and feel you have "more than enough to be comfortable" (as several impact investors have told us), or a foundation wanting to incorporate impact investing into your program strategy (as the Rockefeller Foundation did when it sought to support social service delivery innovation by investing in social impact bonds), you may decide to trade in some financial return for a particular type or intensity of direct impact. If, on the other hand, you want to maximize the financial return on your investments, you might find those opportunities as well. Similarly, if you decide to invest a large portion of your assets for impact, you may be more sensitive to the financial returns they generate than if you invested only a small percentage of your money.

There is no right or wrong choice; it's a matter of constraints and priorities. But determining which category you fit into will help determine which investment path is right for you.

A related consideration is what type of liquidity you need from your impact investments. Are you able to invest money in illiquid assets that cannot (easily) be accessed for a number of years, or will you need to be able to access that capital in the near future? While the bulk of traditional impact investing opportunities have been in long-term private debt or equity, there is an increasing number of more liquid investments from which to choose.

While you're thinking about liquidity, it's also a good idea to start a more nuanced conversation with yourself about the risks you are (or are not) willing to take. As with any investment, articulating your appetite for risk is critical. Investment risk in general is multifaceted. It includes not only the possibility of lower financial returns than you anticipated, but also difficulties in exiting a given investment, fluctuations in currency values (if you are investing overseas), the correlation between any single investment and the rest of your portfolio and other factors. With impact investments, some of these risks might be even greater and additional kinds of risk need to be considered. For example, it's possible that the enterprises you've invested in fail to achieve the social or environmental impact you hoped for, or that measuring this impact proves too challenging.[81] Or, perhaps ironically, you may incur reputational risk if you receive publicity for "making money from poor people." Considering these kinds of risks will help you decide where and how to invest—for example, in early-stage enterprises with new ideas vs established companies with tested business models—and how to mitigate the potential downsides of your investments.

What are your capabilities as an investor? How actively would you like to participate in the allocation and management of your impact investments?

Beyond what matters to you and how you define the types of return you are seeking, it's important to make an honest assessment of your capabilities. Essentially, this comes down to your sophistication as an investor, your knowledge of the areas in which you want to make impact investments, the nature of the financial returns you need or want to generate, the amount of capital you have to work with, and the amount of time you want to devote to impact investing.

A related question to ask yourself is how deeply involved you are going to be in the allocation and management of your impact investments. Are you a sophisticated investor who wants to "roll up your sleeves" and play an active role in making and managing impact investments? If this is the case, you can do so directly, by doing your own research, designating staff to develop expertise in this area (if you have a family office or work for an institution), or hiring an adviser to assist you in identifying a range of opportunities tailored to your needs.

If, on the other hand, you are a sophisticated investor but lack the time needed to take an active role in impact investing—or if you are a new investor and still learning about impact investment terms and concepts—you may want to look for off-the-shelf, "vanilla" products, or hire a wealth manager or adviser to do most of the work needed to build and manage your portfolio.

Unfortunately, what you want to achieve and what you realistically can achieve given your assets, risk tolerance, time, or experience may not always be the same thing. But it's important to identify those gaps ahead of time so you can adjust your expectations and plan accordingly.

You might also want to engage other individuals (perhaps your investment advisers or your children) in the investment process. If so, how do their capabilities compare with your own and what are the practical and financial implications of involving them in your impact investment strategy?

What evidence do you want of the social or environmental returns on your investments?

As we've seen in chapter 4, "Support Systems," new ways of measuring the social and environmental impact of investments are emerging. As an impact investor, you need to think about the level of detail you will require on the difference your investments are making to communities or natural resources. For example, you might only want to invest in enterprises or funds that have been rated by the GIIRS.

Another thing to consider is how much you care about the stories behind the investments, the people whose lives you are affecting. In some cases, you will have opportunities for site visits that will allow you to gain firsthand knowledge of the work you are investing in, and the impact it is achieving.

Taking the Next Steps

As we have just explained, figuring out the best paths for you means first thinking carefully about what you hope to achieve with your investments and what time and resources you have to devote to this part of your portfolio. Your answers to the questions we've posed—about your purpose, your competencies, your level of involvement, and your risk appetite—will help you narrow down the potential investment opportunities from which you can choose. However, options available to you depend not only on your goals and capabilities, but also on the type of investor you are.

Most funds are open only to qualified or accredited investors. On the other hand, they are often too small for consideration by pension funds or other large institutional investors. The latter may prefer the largest and most commercial of private equity funds, or investments in "big ticket" items such as affordable housing or sanitation infrastructure. Meanwhile, smaller (retail) investors generally need to look at investment opportunities that have achieved the highest possible forms of regulatory approval. Fortunately, the diversity of impact investing means that options are available to most of the individuals and institutions who want to participate.

In the following sections, we break down the different ways of getting started in impact investing, depending on the type of investor you are, whether an institution with a sustainability agenda or an individual with a passion to change the world.

Retail Investors

For individuals who want to engage in impact investing but do not have sufficient assets to be considered qualified investors, the options have traditionally been limited. They are quickly expanding, however. One of the easiest things to do is to consider moving money into a CDFI (community development financial institution, which provides credit and financial services to underserved markets and populations) in the form of a CD or other deposit. In the United States, these deposits are federally insured in amounts up to $250,000.

Another possibility is to invest in the growing range of note (debt) products available to retail investors. The first of these was the Calvert Foundation's Community Investment Notes, which for years allowed retail investors to make loans at varying interest rates both within and outside the United States. Calvert is not alone, however. Community Capital Management, a registered investment adviser located in Florida, offers two impact investing mutual funds, the CRA Qualified Investment Fund Retail Shares and the CCM Alternative Income Fund, in addition to tailored services for individual investors. These funds are designed to resemble mainstream fixed-income products while targeting impact objectives, such as supporting affordable housing, job creation, small business development, and environmentally sustainable initiatives.

Enterprise Community Partners offers a note that enables qualified investors to invest as little as $5,000 in affordable housing. The Nature Conservancy's Conservation Note (mentioned in chapter 2, "Who Are the Impact Investors?") allows investors to invest in the preservation of natural resources. In fact, many of the most "vanilla" products are available to retail investors. Also available to retail investors are certificates of deposit and promissory notes offered by Boston-based Trillium Asset Management, which provides capital to CDFIs and nonprofit organizations.

While the products just described are all structured (put together and managed) by investment professionals, new technology platforms have opened up opportunities for individuals to invest directly in other individuals or small enterprises. Some of these peer-to-peer (or P2P) platforms, such as Lending Club, tend to be used for purely profit-making purposes, and their loans would not be considered impact investments. Others are more targeted in purpose, and might be considered impact investments. The firm SoFi, for example, allows accredited investors to lend to students, helping tackle the growing problem of student debt. Perhaps the best-known P2P tool for impact investing is Kiva, which allows individuals to lend as little as $25 to microfinance clients around the world. The borrowers are, in practice, vetted through the microfinance institutions Kiva works with, but direct contact is established between the lender and borrowers. Unlike Lending Club, which offers lenders rates of return as high as 20 percent,[82] Kiva offers a return of principal.

Recent legislation in the United States is broadening the range of opportunities available to retail investors. Previously, "crowdfunding" for start-up businesses or projects could take the form only of loans (as in the case of the P2P sites just described) or grant funding (as in the case of Kickstarter or Indiegogo). In the United States, rules have been proposed by the Securities and Exchanges Commission (SEC) as part of the Jumpstart Our Business Startups (JOBS) Act to allow unaccredited individual investors to invest in certain companies (including impact enterprises) seeking to raise up to $1 million a year (currently, companies can solicit only accredited investors).[83] In the United Kingdom, the Financial Conduct Authority is also developing regulations that make crowdfunding more accessible.[84] While the rules have yet to be fully defined, the changes suggest that with the power of the Internet and the passions of individuals, new crowdfunding opportunities could lead to the increasing democratization of impact investing.

High-Net-Worth Individuals

High-net-worth individuals (a diverse group, but defined here as individuals or couples with at least $1 million in investable assets) have more latitude and more alternatives than many other types of impact investors. For one, they are "qualified investors," meaning they are generally legally able to invest in private debt and equity offerings, which are unavailable to retail investors. For another, they control their own assets, and are thus free from the fiduciary duty constraints that bind institutional investors. And they are generally able to deploy meaningful chunks of their capital into companies and funds that are identified as impact investments. So it is not surprising that they have been at the forefront of much of the innovation that has taken place in impact investing.

Because of the many opportunities available to you, as a high-net-worth investor, it is perhaps most important to articulate your goals and capabilities using some of the questions we posed earlier in this chapter. The next step would likely be to talk to your current wealth manager about your interest and ask what products he or she can suggest.

Here, unfortunately, is where a number of investors get stuck. Few mainstream wealth managers and financial advisers are knowledgeable about impact investing, and most are unaware of the opportunities available to their clients. Some may be outright skeptical of anything that muddies the waters of short-term profitability, either because they are committed philosophically to the "purity" of the profit motive or because their own compensation structure is not well served by these types of investments. A 2012 study suggested that male wealth managers and those who have been in the business longer are less likely to respond positively to client interest in impact investing than their female or younger counterparts.[85]

Whatever the reason, if you have found your wealth manager unresponsive, you are not alone. We often hear investors express this frustration. One young woman, who encountered pushback from her family's wealth manager when she wanted to move the assets in her trust into impact investments, emphasized the need for investors to press for what they want. "We all need to remember that financial advisers work for us," she said. "People don't think they can ask for clarifications, or push back, or say they don't understand. People are worried about exerting the authority they have, but it's their money and they have ultimate say."

Even if your adviser is unresponsive to your inquiry, client demand may encourage him or her to learn more about this area—so we urge you to be persistent in your requests. In recent years, the barrier posed by large institutional wealth managers seems to be rapidly breaking down. And some of the world's largest and most mainstream asset managers (including Morgan Stanley, Goldman Sachs, and BlackRock) have announced the creation of products or managed accounts to serve clients interested in impact investing. As others follow their lead, you may well find you can pursue your interest in this area through your existing manager. If you hit a brick wall, however, it may be valuable to engage one of a growing number of specialized managers and advisers in this area. For example, the young woman who encountered pushback from her family's traditional wealth manager moved her assets to San Francisco-based asset manager Sonen Capital because she feels its principals "understand where I am coming from, and my values. I can rely on them to tell me what is possible and what is not possible, given the structures I am working with." Helene Marsh, whom we met in chapter 2, trusts New York–based Veris Wealth Partners to manage her assets.

Other specialist advisers and managers in the United States include Imprint Capital, the CapRock Group, Trillium Asset Management, and Wetherby Asset Management. These firms have different approaches and strengths, so you may want to inquiries at more than one. Questions to ask any of them might include:

- What is the general approach they take with new clients? How do they manage their ongoing relationships with clients?
- What is the impact focus of most of the investments they make on behalf of their clients—environmental or social, domestic or international, targeted or general?
- What range of financial return expectations do their clients have? What opportunities do they provide for liquid versus nonliquid investments?
- What is the range of asset sizes they manage for clients? What is the minimum size?
- What fees do they charge, and how are they compensated?
- How does the firm measure and report on the social and environmental impact of clients' impact investments?
- How do they approach the integrated management of clients' impact and traditional investments?

You may also want to speak with existing clients of the firm about their experiences. We have found a great level of openness among impact investors, and a desire to be helpful to others.

Finally, if you are a savvy investor, you may want to roll up your sleeves and investigate the possibility of making direct investments—either in addition to or in place of a consultation. This can be a simple or complex exercise, depending on your goals and capabilities. A number of structured products exist to facilitate easy participation, with terms that look similar to standard investments. The most "vanilla" of these are often available to retail investors, as described in the Retail Investors section in this chapter. A number of funds are available only to accredited investors, however. The GIIN's ImpactBase includes profiles of dozens of funds that are raising capital in the form of debt, equity, or a combination of the two, in a wide range of sectors and geographies. Registration on ImpactBase is free, and available to all accredited investors.

It is advisable to roll up your sleeves, however, only if you are an experienced investor. Even then, these investments (like almost all investments) come with the risk of loss. Andrew Kassoy, an individual impact investor with 15 years' experience in mainstream private equity, was surprised to receive notice that one of his investees, the fund E+Co, had written down over 40 percent of its investments in small clean energy businesses in emerging markets. Subsequent analysis revealed deep flaws in the fund's management and practices, weaknesses of which Kassoy had been unaware at the time of his investment.

When reflecting on what he would have done differently, and what differentiated E+Co from his successful investments in comparable funds such as Root Capital, Kassoy highlighted the role of due diligence. "It is tempting to make decisions based on emotions, given the compelling missions of the companies and funds in this space," he says. "But you need to be careful not to let that interfere with actual investment diligence."

Conducting some of this due diligence is relatively straightforward. For example, you can look at the experience and skills of the fund management team. Some analysis is a little more complicated, such as gaining an understanding of a fund's underlying drivers of cost, value creation, and cash flow. In the case of E+Co, investors were being promised 7 percent net returns on a debt fund that was used to make equity investments in its underlying businesses, small and illiquid clean energy companies across Africa, Asia, and Latin America.

"If you think about what would have been required from portfolio companies in order to provide investors the return we were promised, the math didn't add up," says Kassoy. "Root Capital promises a more realistic 2 percent return on its debt note, which is used to make short-term loans to farmers to get them through a growing season." However, another part of what caused E+Co to fail, he explains, was its poor systems and internal controls, which stand in sharp contrast to the substantial investment in management information systems made by Root Capital. As a prospective investor doing your own due diligence, it is very difficult to look under the hood at the systems and controls in place. Kassoy noted, however, that this challenge is often true for mainstream as well as impact investments.

If you are confident in your ability to do due diligence and comfortable with the risk involved, you may even want to go a step further and consider direct investments. If so, you can join one of the angel investor networks that have a dedicated focus on impact investing. These networks (which include Toniic and Investors' Circle) provide access to some of the most innovative and promising start-ups. Like their mainstream counterparts, they also often provide support for the enterprises that receive investment.

The benefits of participating in angel networks are numerous. For one, they provide access to a pipeline of viable investments and the opportunity to share the due diligence that staff or members have done on those investments—work that, done alone, would be costly and difficult, particularly for enterprises located in developing countries or in remote rural areas. Toniic members, for example, review more than 200 global impact deals a year, mostly in developing countries. Members of Investors' Circle can access local investor networks, participate in in-person and virtual venture fairs, use the network's online resources, receive deal updates, and access more than 500 deals a year. They can also preview new deals and tap into the expertise and experience of others by being part of selection committees.

Joining these networks allows you not only to access prescreened deals but also to tap into the knowledge and expertise of others. This is something François de Borchgrave likes about being a member of Toniic. "What's very important is gaining learning and experience from other people and experience of sectors, geographies, and deal structure that I'd not otherwise be familiar with," he says.

Most networks offer workshops, online events, conferences, and members' meetings and lunches. Toniic, for example, has run events focusing on impact investing in regions such as Latin America and India. It has also published an online e-guide on investing in early-stage impact enterprises that discusses the difference between impact investing and other investing and describes how to become a practitioner using a seven-step framework.

You need not join an existing network, however; you can form your own. Seattle-based Shaula Massena, for example, joined with nine other small-scale impact investors in the Seattle region, each of whom contributed $10,000, to form an impact angel fund. The fund was an outgrowth of a discussion group Massena and a friend had started on the topic of community impact investing. Massena had already made an investment through Investors' Circle, and appreciated the value of that larger national network, but she also wanted to build relationships, learn by doing, and get closer to her investments as well as to like-minded fellow investors. The Seattle group filtered out larger deals being considered by other angel groups because they wanted a more personal connection with their investments. Massena explains: "We wanted to be able to look each other in the eye and figure out whether the deals we were looking at were truly impactful."

Among the group's early investments is a $50,000 loan they are negotiating with Viva Farms, a nonprofit organization that helps incubate small scale farms. The loan has enabled Viva to acquire new machinery (cooling equipment) that will increase farmers' sales by extending the shelf life of their produce, thereby reducing waste and increasing margins. Massena explains: "We could clearly see how the loan would be repaid, and how it would have impact."

Family Offices

Individuals or families with substantial net worth may invest it through a family or multifamily office or other captive investment company. If you are among the small number of people who fall into this category, you have the same opportunities available to high-net-worth investors plus some additional ones. Whereas most individual investors (notwithstanding those who make direct investments) are passive investors, who are generally limited to the existing universe of products or funds, family offices usually operate at a scale that justifies having the staff to take a more active role in crafting larger investments. Capricorn Investment Group, for example, directly employs teams to manage a dozen proprietary or semiproprietary funds as well as the underlying investments of those funds.

Family offices generally approach their investments with a multi-generational time horizon, which enables them to provide a patient source of capital if they so choose. Most also have the discretion and sophistication to select from a diverse range of impact investing strategies, including new and therefore relatively risky types of investment, and to evolve them over time in response to ongoing learning and changes in the market. Charles Ewald, CEO and CIO of New Island Capital Management in San Francisco, explains that his firm has undergone a long process of learning and adaptation since it was founded eight years ago. In the beginning, it had a mandate to identify "late-stage ventures that would produce top-quartile returns as well as substantial impact," but found that this approach precluded a lot of the deals the firm would like to have done. Over time, Ewald explains, "we realized we were really called upon to earn a sustainable rate of return, not necessarily a fully loaded market rate of return (when you take into account the risk). When we made that shift, it allowed us to grow the team and freed us up to fill an investment gap."

If you have or are starting a family office, you could begin by discussing your interests with staff and dedicating one or more members of your team to exploring the universe of potential impact investments. You may look to existing family offices with expertise in impact investing (such as New Island Capital Management or the RS Group in Hong Kong) for examples of how others have approached the deployment of assets into impact investments. These examples range from those with a mandate to "outperform the market" to those with a mandate to generate a more flexible, "sustainable" rate of return. You may find it useful to participate in one of the growing number of forums held for family offices, many of which have introduced sessions on impact investing. Once you are ready to commit, you might elect to hire new staff dedicated to this type of investing, launch an RFP (request for proposal) to subcontract the management of a portion of your assets to a dedicated wealth management firm, or join forces with similarly minded families and individuals.

Institutional Investors

If you represent an institutional investor and want to pursue new opportunities within your mandate, it is also useful to begin by articulating your goals and assessing your capabilities and constraints. The specifics of this process will depend on the dynamics at play within the institution, including who is initiating the interest and which stakeholders are being consulted.

One way of starting is to conduct a survey of staff and/or clients to get a sense of their interest. In parallel, you could review existing capabilities and assets within the existing business to find out which of these you might be able to tap into as you develop an impact investing strategy. Questions to ask yourself and your colleagues might include:

- Do you see impact investing as a way of meeting new client interest and, if so, what kinds of opportunities are your clients demanding?
- Is impact investing an extension of your SRI activities, such as clean-tech investment or screened fund offerings?
- Is impact investing a means of meeting regulatory obligations such as those in the Community Reinvestment Act?
- On the flip side, does your impact investing activity need to comply with regulations or accounting guidelines that limit the universe of potential impact investments?
- Do you want your organization and brand to be seen as a pioneer in this emerging area of investment practice?
- What resources and knowledge about impact investing does your organization have internally?

To get started, it is a good idea to dedicate a staff person or working group to consult with the growing range of resources (e.g., GIIN). In a number of institutions including BlackRock, such a team emerged organically from staff interest. In others, it might be appointed.

For banks, the entry points for impact investing vary widely. JPMorgan Chase's J.P. Morgan Social Sector Finance unit, for example, sits at the corporate bank, while UBS's Values-Based Investing unit was created within its private bank. Goldman Sachs's impact investing activity, including its pioneering work on social impact bonds (SIBs), originated in its Urban Investment Group, an investing team that was established to deploy balance sheet capital and later assumed the Firm's obligations under the Community Reinvestment Act when it became a bank holding company. More recently, the group has expanded to include a third party fund offering in response to interest from clients of the private bank.

If institutions' approach to impact investing crosses multiple lines of business, it may be helpful to establish a dedicated champion within the organization to coordinate activities.

Take a look at your existing capabilities to see if they can be aligned with impact investing. Prudential Financial's $400 million Social Investments portfolio, for example, builds on the institution's strengths as a debt investor. If your institution is already engaged in related investments, such as clean technology investing or socially responsible investment, it may be that your impact investing could build upon them. If your institution is a signatory to the United Nations' Principles for Responsible Investment (UNPRI),[86] it has access to a one-stop shop for responsible investing, as UNPRI offers advice and support on how to incorporate sustainability into investment decisions and ownership practices. UNPRI has been exploring impact investing through workshops and roundtable events that bring together investors and academics.

Foundations

Impact investing allows foundations to advance their social or environmental missions while generating a return that can be put back into the organization's programs or investments. In the United States, this can be done through a variety of strategies on "either side of the house" (through a foundation's endowment, its program budget, or both), but the approach will vary depending on which options are chosen as the route into impact investing. Outside the United States, the distinction between a foundation's corpus and its annual charitable spending may be quite different.

As we saw in chapter 2, "Who Are the Impact Investors?" foundations active in impact investing can also use program-related investments (PRIs) as a tool for advancing their charitable mission.

PRIs were created as a type of investment in the tax regulations in the 1970s to allow foundations to invest in what might otherwise be "jeopardizing investments" due to the riskiness or low returns. Foundations are subject to penalty taxes on investments that jeopardize their ability to meet their charitable purposes and are not "prudent." (There are prudency standards at the individual state level as well.) An investment can be treated as a PRI and not a jeopardy investment if the primary purpose for making it is charitable, the production of income is not a significant reason for the investment (as shown through the downside such as high risk, low return along with illiquidity) and the funds are not used for political or lobbying purposes. An investment that is a PRI qualifies toward a foundation's 5 percent annual charitable payout, and when the principal amount is repaid or recovered, the foundation's payout is increased by that recovery or repayment. Income earned during the life of the PRI is taxable, along with the foundation's other investment income at 1 or 2 percent per year.

Alternatively, or additionally, foundations can make impact investments from their corpus or endowment. Unlike PRIs, these investments do not have a specific legal definition and are generally referred to as mission-related investing (MRIs) or mission-driven investing. Like PRIs, MRIs are made to achieve social or environmental impact objectives while producing a financial return. Unlike PRIs, however, MRIs do not count as charitable expenditures toward a foundation's annual payout requirements. They still must be prudent and reasonable within the foundation's investment policy and are generally designed to help preserve its assets through the generation of competitive financial returns. Like PRIs, they can take a number of forms, including debt, real estate, private equity, or venture capital.

When considering how your foundation might approach impact investing, here are some questions to ask:

- Do you think of impact investments as an additional tool in your philanthropic toolkit, a way to activate more of the foundation's assets for impact, or both?
- Is there an individual on the foundation's staff who has the skills necessary to perform financial and social due diligence, and to structure and manage investments?
- Can you combine these skills by forming a team of staff from different divisions?

- Does your endowment manager (whether internal or external) have experience, or willingness, to make impact investments?
- Will this require hiring an additional staff member and/or outside adviser?

As other types of investors do, your foundation might find it useful to consult with an outside adviser to formulate a strategy and operational plan, and/or to make or monitor investments. If you are interested in making impact investments with the corpus and already use a third-party endowment manager, your first step might be to inquire about the current manager's capabilities.

When looking to build your knowledge of impact investing, you can choose from a number of resources that serve foundations' needs. Conducting a search for "mission investing" brings up a range of resources, from white papers to news from other foundations. The Mission Investors Exchange is among the most prominent, since it focuses all its activities in this area. The organization's website offers a range of resources, from a glossary of terms, to links to related websites, details of training events and workshops, and advice on topics such how to start a mission investor program or measure its impact.

Meanwhile, organizations set up to offer foundations a broad range of resources are increasingly developing research papers and guides focused on MRIs, PRIs and impact investing. The Foundation Center, for instance, has produced fact sheets on mission investing, downloadable from the "Gain Knowledge" section of its website. Confluence Philanthropy, a network of more than 200 philanthropic institutions, exists to provide technical support and resources to those seeking to deploy their assets in pursuit of positive environmental impact and social justice.

Another online resource is GrantCraft, a project of the Foundation Center and the European Foundation Centre, was established to offer "practical wisdom for funders." GrantCraft offers a range of guides, podcasts, videos, and case studies, including content on

PRIs. In addition, Rockefeller Philanthropy Advisors has produced two useful monographs on the topic of impact investing among foundations.

Where to Go Next

Deciding on your impact investment strategy may require doing some research into the impact investing universe and the different options available. This is true whether you are an individual, a foundation, or an institution.

Fortunately, a growing set of resources exists. These include written material produced by foundations such as the Rockefeller Foundation (of which this book is just one), but also by banks such as JPMorgan Chase and Morgan Stanley and by philanthropy advisers such as Rockefeller Philanthropy Advisors and Arabella Advisors. When it comes to local investment, local community foundations are rich sources of information on the different options. The Resources section of this book also provides some useful documents and tools. Much of this information is just a click away. The Resources section of the GIIN's website features a wide range of research papers, for example. Moreover, increasingly, specialist investment advisers are producing, and posting on their websites, guides and brochures to increase their clients' knowledge of impact investing in a range of areas, from climate change to affordable housing. Other resources include databases such as the ImpactAssets 50, an annual showcase of impact investment fund managers; or GIIN's ImpactBase, a global online directory of impact investment vehicles.

Another effective way of absorbing information is to attend a workshop or conference on impact investing (an online search quickly pulls up some of the leading events). Conferences and workshops offer not only knowledge and insights from expert speakers but also a chance to meet like-minded individuals and institutions and find out how they embarked on impact investing, what challenges they've faced, and what the rewards have been. As is true when building up knowledge on anything, it is often in these informal conversations that the most powerful lessons are learned.

Some people may prefer to read extensively about impact investing before putting a toe in the water, while others prefer to learn by doing. The choice of which direction to take will depend on factors ranging from your level of knowledge to your appetite for risk. Plenty of resources and opportunities exist to support a wide variety of approaches. Whatever path you decide to take, the journey should start with an articulation of your goals and capabilities. After that, the most important thing is to dive in and get started. The sooner you do, the sooner you and your investments will be able to play a role in solving the world's most pressing social and environmental problems.

Epilogue

In this book we hope we have shown you why and how impact investing is proving a compelling idea with promising results thus far. As we have demonstrated, the community of impact investors, from individuals and private bankers to institutional investors and foundation heads, is expanding. Not surprisingly, they are hungry for knowledge as they incorporate impact investment into their wealth management or philanthropic strategies. An ecosystem of advisers, networks, and measurement tools is rapidly evolving, too. The question is whether this wave of enthusiasm and groundswell of activity mark the birth of a new era in which people, and the planet, become an integral part of investment decisions. We believe it does.

So what would happen if impact investing were to become part of "business as usual"? Let's do a little future gazing.

Imagine that in 2030, an individual investor (we'll call him Luis Sanchez) wakes up one morning to the news that an immense storm (one even more devastating than Typhoon Haiyan, which smashed across the Philippines in November 2013) has hit Bangladesh. Luis has for many years been allocating roughly 10 percent of his investment portfolio to impact investments that focus on improving early childhood education in the United States, something he sees as critical to building a prosperous, equitable society. However, when he visited some rural areas while on a business trip to Asia, it brought home to Luis, a New York commercial real estate manager, how basic the conditions remain for so many people living in developing countries. Now watching images of flattened homes and people desperately seeking food and shelter, he wants to use some of his investments to help these communities become more resilient in the face of the growing effects of climate change.

Approaching his investment adviser, Luis finds that she can suggest a number of options. He could invest in a start-up that is providing affordable building materials to communities in parts of the world particularly badly affected by storms and climate change. The company's products incorporate new materials that can withstand strong winds and rain and are sold in custom-designed modules using 3D printers, allowing families to transform flimsy wooden structures into more resilient homes, piece by piece. Alternatively, he could put his money into a fund focused on enterprises that are developing a range of climate adaptation technologies, from wetland restoration methods to advance-warning systems. The fund has recently been delivering modest but steady returns for its investors. While Luis is excited by the idea of 3D-printed homes for low-income communities, he decides that because he needs a predictable rate of return from his investments, he will invest in the climate adaptation fund.

Now let's imagine that in 2030 a woman dies the year after her husband dies—we'll call them Jane and John Smith—leaving their two children in charge of the family foundation the couple established 50 years earlier. The foundation had been directing funds into nonprofit organizations working to eradicate guinea worm disease. This painful condition arises when, after water containing the fleas is ingested, guinea worm larvae hatch in the digestive tract and emerge from the body, frequently through a person's limbs. Before marrying John and settling down in San Francisco, Jane had spent several years working in parts of Africa where the guinea worm was prevalent, so she had wanted to devote most of their charitable funds to wiping out the disease.

However, in their later years, the couple realized that remarkable progress was being made in combating the guinea worm disease, with the number of cases falling dramatically since the late 1980s, when they set up their foundation. They also watched as their children (both passionate about helping reduce homelessness and its devastating effects on American society) developed very different interests from theirs. As a result, they decided to give the foundation substantial flexibility in how its funds could be distributed. They therefore included a provision in their will that, should they wish to, their children could alter the focus of their grant making.

Once in charge of the foundation, Jo and Rick Smith approached their wealth adviser about how they could use a portion of its endowment to make investments that would further the foundation's goals. They were particularly interested in increasing the availability of affordable housing. The adviser suggested a social impact bond commissioned by the City of Fresno mayor's office to combat homelessness. They put a portion of the foundation's funds into the investment. Since then, it has allowed the siblings to participate in the progress being made on an issue about which they care deeply. The foundation receives returns when there is a measurable cut in the number of street sleepers and a fall in the number of emergency room visits per person per year. With the returns on this and other investments, the foundation continues to generate resources that fund grants to nonprofits testing innovative ways of combating homelessness, some of which may provide well-validated services that will form the basis for new SIBs to come.

Finally, imagine that in 2030 a large US pension fund invests in the installation of distributed renewable energy infrastructure in affordable housing complexes and other large facilities. These micro-grids allow residents to use renewable energy that is generated on site, thereby reducing their monthly utility bills, lessening their vulnerability to power outages during natural disasters and eliminating their contribution to fossil fuel emissions. In addition to getting a fixed rate of return on its investment, the pension fund was attracted to the investment because it creates high-quality jobs for local residents, many of which are clients of the pension fund.

Today, while these three scenarios are becoming more common, they are not yet the norm. Not every retail investor has access to an adviser who can offer a range of impact investing products. Not every impact fund can find a social impact bond that will advance its particular mission while also generating returns. Not every pension fund can identify viable infrastructure investments that generate local jobs and fight climate change. Millions of investors are not yet aware that impact investing is an option for them.

But imagine if these kinds of impact investment choices were well known and easy to make, with options available to meet everyone's goals, with wealth managers and others well equipped to advise on the best choices, and with a range of user-friendly measurement tools allowing easy tracking of the impact of each investment. Imagine if prevailing norms, or even tax benefits, allowed an allocation to impact investing in the way they prescribe philanthropic contributions, and if long-term environmental and social impacts were factored into all investment decisions. Imagine if substantial portions of our global financial resources were devoted to making the world a better place. This would be a world in which entrepreneurial ideas for addressing big global problems could easily access injections of private capital, which would give those ideas a good chance (the same chance as any start-up) of becoming enterprises and systems capable of bringing about transformational change in everything from health care and homelessness to natural conservation.

Here's where you come in. Every time you wonder about the relationship between your investments and the social or environmental problems you most care about, and make an inquiry with a wealth manager or have a discussion with a colleague or a friend about it, you are advancing prospects for impact investing. Every time you take the plunge and make an impact investment, you do even more to expand the pool of impact investors and help this form of investing take root. And the more investors that get behind this growing movement, the more likely it is not only to have a large-scale social and environmental impact but also to become a form of investing that is highly attractive from a financial standpoint.

Of course, for some, impact investing will be a small part of how they use their money to contribute to social change. For others, it will be a major focus of their capital deployments. Impact investing allows investors to challenge long-standing orthodoxies about capitalism—or simply to produce incremental benefits within their existing activities. As we have seen, there is plenty of room for a wide range of approaches and worldviews. But all of them are based on a powerful idea: that this form of investing has the potential to bring about widespread change by harnessing the power of capital markets.

To be part of this exciting new investment ecosystem, you will need a range of resources. You'll need to do further research, to find out who can best advise you, and start discussions with everyone from friends and family to colleagues, clients, and shareholders. You might join an angel network. Many investors have already enthusiastically embraced this form of investing. To those early pioneers, we salute you and thank you, and we encourage you to persist in your work. And for those who have yet to embark on this journey, we hope this book will provide the impetus needed to get you started. When you do, you will become part of an investment approach that can feed your passions, help meet your financial goals, and unlock workable capital that can expand dramatically the resources available to those working to address the world's biggest problems.

Acknowledgments

First, our sincere gratitude to Sarah Murray for serving as senior editor—this book would be just a twinkle in our eyes without her thoughtful collaboration and expert wordsmithing.

Our equally sincere thanks goes to the communications team at the Rockefeller Foundation, especially Neill Coleman, Traci Carpenter, and Laura Gordon. And to the entire Rockefeller Foundation impact investing team, past and present, especially Antony Bugg-Levine, Brinda Ganguly, Justina Lai, Rehana Nathoo, Andrea Porter, and Kelly Teevan. Their hard work and leadership have been instrumental in the success stories that we're able to tell through this publication.

In addition, we are deeply grateful to the many impact investors and entrepreneurs who shared their perspectives and experiences with us—without their talent and passion, none of this would be possible and we are so inspired by your example. We would like especially to acknowledge the many wonderful grantees and partners of the Foundation's impact investing initiative, and in particular our core partners like the Global Impact Investing Network (GIIN), B Lab and its Global Impact Investing Rating System (GIIRS), the Impact Investing Policy Collaborative and Social Finance.

To our editorial and publishing team at Wharton Digital Press—Steve Kobrin, Shannon Berning, and Teresa Kocudak—who believed in this ebook from the beginning and whose insights and close reading have challenged us, as well as cheered us.

To our publicist, Whitney Peeling, for helping us to reach new, important audiences. We believe that the growth and success of impact investing is not just about getting people to invest more, but getting more people to invest period, so thank you.

To the team at the Center for High Impact Philanthropy at the University of Pennsylvania for approaching us to write this book and offering early thought-partnership.

Finally, to our family and friends who have encouraged us, read early drafts, and provided counsel along the way—we love and thank you.

Resources

Acumen Fund
www.acumen.org

Ashoka
www.ashoka.org

The Aspen Network of Development Entrepreneurs
www.aspeninstitute.org/policy-work/aspen-network-development-
entrepreneurs

BALLE
https://bealocalist.org

B Analytics
http://b-analytics.net

B Lab
www.bcorporation.net

Confluence Philanthropy
www.confluencephilanthropy.org

Echoing Green
www.echoinggreen.org

Global Impact Investing Network (GIIN)
www.thegiin.org

Global Impact Investing Ratings System (GIIRS)
http://giirs.org

GrantCraft
www.grantcraft.org

ImpactBase
www.impactbase.org

Impact Reporting and Investment Standards (IRIS)
http://iris.thegiin.org

Indian Angel Network
www.indianangelnetwork.com

Investors' Circle
www.investorscircle.net

Mission Investors Exchange
www.missioninvestors.org

Mission Markets
www.missionmarkets.com

Sankalp Forum
www.sankalpforum.com

Sistema B
www.sistemab.org

Toniic
www.toniic.com

United Nations Principles for Responsible Investment (UNPRI)
www.unpri.org/prian-events/impact-investing

Further Reading

Alto, Philo. "Impact Investing: Will Hype Stall Its Emergence as an Asset Class?" *Social Space*, 2012. https://centres.smu.edu.sg/wp-content/uploads/2013/09/SocialSpace2012-PhiloAlto.pdf.

Avantage Ventures Asia Pacific Impact Investment Report. "Impact Investing in Asia: The Opportunities, the Challenges, and Where It Is Headed.": Asia Pacific Impact Investment Report. http://s3.amazonaws.com/zanran_storage/www.avantageventures.com/ContentPages/2500714485.pdf.

Brest, Paul, and Kelly Born. "When Can Impact Investing Create Real Impact?" *Stanford Social Innovation Review* (Fall 2013). http://www.ssireview.org/up_for_debate/article/impact_investing.

Clark, Cathy, Jed Emerson, and Ben Thornley. "Impact Investing 2.0: The Way Forward." http://www.pacificcommunityventures.org/impinv2/.

Dalberg Global Development Advisors. "Impact Investing in West Africa." April 2011. http://www.rockefellerfoundation.org/blog/impact-investing-west-africa.

Emerson, Jed. "Risk, Return and Impact: Understanding Diversification and Performance within an Impact Investing Portfolio." ImpactAssets brief. http://www.impactassets.org/files/downloads/ImpactAssets_IssueBriefs_2.pdf.

Emerson, Jed, and Antony Bugg-Levine. *Impact Investing: Transforming How We Make Money While Making a Difference.* Hoboken, NJ: Jossey-Bass, 2011.

"From the Margins to the Mainstream: Assessment of the Impact Investment Sector and Opportunities to Engage Mainstream Investors." World Economic Forum, September 2013. http://www3.weforum.org/docs/WEF_II_FromMarginsMainstream_Report_2013.pdf.

"Gateways to Impact: Industry Survey of Financial Advisors on Sustainable and Impact Investing." June 2012. http://www.gatewaystoimpact.org/images/gatewaystoimpact.pdf.

Hope Consulting. "Money for Good: Impact Investing Overview." 2010. http://www.hopeconsulting.us/pdf/Money_for_Good_Impact_Investing_Overview.pdf.

J.P. Morgan. "Insight into the Impact Investment Market: An In-Depth Analysis of Investor Perspectives and over 2,200 Transactions." J.P. Morgan Social Finance, Global Impact Investing Network, Social Finance Research. December 14, 2011. http://www.thegiin.org/cgi-bin/iowa/download?row=334&field=gated_download_1.

J.P. Morgan and the Rockefeller Foundation. "Impact Investments: An Emerging Asset Class." 2010. http://www.rockefellerfoundation.org/uploads/files/2b053b2b-8feb-46ea-adbd-f89068d59785-impact.pdf.

J.P. Morgan Global Impact Investing Network. "Perspectives on Progress: The Impact Investor Survey." January 2013. http://www.jpmorganchase.com/corporate/socialfinance/document/130107_Perspectives_on_Progress.pdf.

Karamchandani, Ashish, Michael Kubzansky, and Paul Frandano (Monitor Group). "Emerging Markets, Emerging Models: Market-Based Solutions to the Challenges of Global Poverty." March 2009. http://www.mim.monitor.com/downloads/emergingmarkets_full.pdf.

Koh, Harvey, Ashish Karamchandani, and Robert Katz (Monitor Group). "From Blueprint to Scale: The Case for Philanthropy in Impact Investing." April 2012. http://www.mim.monitor.com/downloads/Blueprint_To_Scale/From%20Blueprint%20to%20Scale%20-%20Case%20for%20Philanthropy%20in%20Impact%20Investing_Full%20report.pdf.

Pacific Community Ventures, Harvard University, and the Rockefeller Foundation. "Impact at Scale: Policy Innovation for Institutional Investment with Social and Environmental Benefit." February 2012. http://hausercenter.org/iri/wp-content/uploads/2010/05/FINAL_ Impact-at-Scale_InSight_IRI_February-2012_FULL-REPORT.pdf.

Rockefeller Foundation. "Accelerating Impact: Achievements, Challenges and What's Next in Building the Impact Investing Industry." July 2012. http://www.rockefellerfoundation.org/uploads/images/fda23ba9-ab7e-4c83-9218-24fdd79289cc.pdf.

Rockefeller Foundation. "Impact Investing: A Framework for Policy Design and Analysis." 2011. http://www.rockefellerfoundation.org/blog/ impact-investing-framework-policy.

Rockefeller Philanthropy Advisors. "Impact Investing: An Introduction." Philanthropy Roadmap series. https://rockpa.org/document.doc?id=239.

"Solutions for Impact Investors: From Strategy to Implementation." November 2009. http://rockpa.org/document.doc?id=15.

Sonen Capital and the KL Felicitas Foundation. "Evolution of an Impact Portfolio: From Implementation to Results." October 2013. http://www. sonencapital.com/evolution-of-impact.php.

Notes

1 Based on his TEDx talk, at http://www.cordesfoundation.org/ron-cordes-at-tedxsanjoaquin-catalyzing-capital-to-change-the-world/.

2 World Health Organization: http://www.who.int/macrohealth/background/findings/en/index.html.

3 Mapping global capital markets 2011, McKinsey Global Institute, August 2011: http://www.mckinsey.com/insights/global_capital_markets/mapping_global_capital_markets_2011.

4 John J. Havens and Paul G. Schervish, "Why the $41 Trillion Wealth Transfer Estimate Is Still Valid: A Review of Challenges and Questions," Boston College Social Welfare Research Institute, 2003, cited in *From the Margins to the Mainstream, Assessment of the Impact Investment Sector and Opportunities to Engage Mainstream Investors,* report by the World Economic Forum's Mainstreaming Impact Investing initiative, 2013, 1.2 Motivation: http://reports.weforum.org/impact-investment/view/1-introduction-to-the-mainstreaming-impact-investing-initiative/1-2-motivation/.

5 "City of Philadelphia Partners with Liberty United to Reduce Gun Violence," Philadelphia City press release, July 1, 2013, http://cityofphiladelphia.wordpress.com/2013/07/01/city-of-philadelphia-partners-with-liberty-united-to-reduce-gun-violence/.

6 Michael E. Porter and Mark R. Kramer, "Creating Shared Value," *Harvard Business Review,* January 2011, http://hbr.org/2011/01/the-big-idea-creating-shared-value.

7 Rockefeller Foundation, "Accelerating Impact: Achievements, Challenges and What's Next in Building the Impact Investing Industry," July 2012, p. ix, http://www.rockefellerfoundation.org/uploads/images/fda23ba9-ab7e-4c83-9218-24fdd79289cc.pdf.

8 U.S. SIF Foundation, "Report on Sustainable and Responsible Investing Trends in the United States," 2012, http://www.ussif.org/sribasics.

9 Sustainable Capitalism, Generation Investment Management, February 15, 2012: http://www.generationim.com/media/pdf-generation-sustainable-capitalism-v1.pdf.

10 Ceres, "Investors Achieve Strong Results on Climate Change, Supply Chains, Water Risks during 2013 Proxy Season," August 8, 2013, https://www.ceres.org/press/press-releases/investors-achieve-strong-results-on-climate-change-supply-chains-water-risks-during-2013-proxy-season.

11 Michael Blowfield and Alan Murray, "Corporate Responsibility: A Critical Introduction" (New York: Oxford University Press, 2008), p. 292; and Stanford Graduate School of Business case study, at https://gsbapps.stanford.edu/cases/documents/SI73.pdf.

12 Christine W. Letts, William Ryan, and Alan Grossman, "Virtuous Capital: What Foundations Can Learn from Venture Capitalists," *Harvard Business Review*, 1997, http://www.wheatridge.org/wp-content/uploads/2012/03/Virtuous_Capital_HB.pdf.

13 d.light website: http://www.dlightdesign.com/impact-dashboard/.

14 Rockefeller Foundation, "Accelerating Impact: Achievements, Challenges and What's Next in Building the Impact Investing Industry," July 2012, p. 16, http://www.rockefellerfoundation.org/uploads/images/fda23ba9-ab7e-4c83-9218-24fdd79289cc.pdf.

15 Kellogg Foundation website: http://www.wkkf.org/what-we-do/featured-work/ncb-capital-impact.

16 Pritzker, Goldman Sachs Announce $20 Million First Phase of Early Childhood Innovation Accelerator Initiative, ImprintCapital press release, 2013: http://www.imprintcap.com/2013/06/pritzker-goldman-sachs-announce-20-million-first-phase-of-early-childhood-innovation-accelerator-initiative/.

17 Hope Consulting, "Money for Good: Impact Investing Overview," 2010, p. 7, http://www.hopeconsulting.us/pdf/Money_for_Good_Impact_Investing_Overview.pdf.

18 4-traders website: http://www.4-traders.com/UBS-AG-9365071/news/UBS-AG-UBS-launches-first-fund-for-Impact-Investing-17288728/.

19 "Zurich Invests up to USD 1 Billion to Help Communities Adapt to Climate Change," Zurich Insurance Group press release, November 18, 2013, http://www.zurich.com/media/newsreleases/2013/2013-1118-01.htm.

20 CalPERS California Initiative 2011: Creating Opportunities in California's Underserved Markets, CalPERS website: http://www.calpers.ca.gov/eip-docs/investments/targeted-programs/2011-ca-initiative.pdf.

21 PGGM website: http://www.pggm.nl/wat-vinden-we/Paginas/7-inzichten-in-impact-beleggen.aspx; Asset Allocation CIO: http://ai-cio.com/channel/ASSET_ALLOCATION/PGGM's_Seven_Steps_to_Impact_Investing.html.

22 Antony Elliott, "Investing for the Good of Society: Why and How Wealthy Individuals Respond," The FairBanking Foundation, http://www.nesta.org.uk/library/documents/BSFFGoodofSocietyprint.pdf.

23 Deloitte, *The Millennial Survey 2013*, p. 5, http://www2.deloitte.com/content/dam/Deloitte/global/Documents/About-Deloitte/dttl-crs-millennial-innovation-survey-2013.pdf.

24 Greyston website: http://greyston.com/the-bakery-open-hiring/.

25 Acumen Fund website: http://acumen.org/investment/lifespring/.

26 Ashoka website: https://www.ashoka.org/fellow/gonzalo-muñoz.

27 Sustainable Harvest website: http://www.sustainableharvest.com/about/.

28 "LeapFrog Investments Raises over $200m for Emerging Consumer Fund, as Insurers and Asset Managers Tap New Source of Growth and Profits," *PR Newswire*, September 9, 2013, http://www.prnewswire.com/news-releases/leapfrog-investments-raises-over-200m-for-emerging-consumer-fund-as-insurers-and-asset-managers-tap-new-source-of-growth-and-profits-222940711.html.

29 Boston Community Capital website: http://www.bostoncommunitycapital.org/who.

30 Boston Community Capital website: http://www.bostoncommunitycapital.org/what/loan-fund.

31 Aavishkaar Venture Management Services, "Aavishkaar II: Building Bharat Sustainably," 2010, p. 3.

32 "SEIIF, Oxfam, and Symbiotics target investment industry with a new SME fund," January 21, 2012, Symbiotics website: http://www.symbioticsgroup.com/news/latest-news/seiif-oxfam-and-symbiotics-target-investment-industry-with-new-sme-fund.

33 5 Stone Green Capital LLC, "Center/West: Investment Committee Memorandum," August 10, 2013.

34 Lyme Timber Company website: http://www.lymetimber.com/.

35 Nature Conservancy website: http://www.nature.org/about-us/conservation-note.xml.

36 UK Cabinet Office, April 2013: http://data.gov.uk/sib_knowledge_box/ministry-justice-offenders-released-peterborough-prison.

37 Ministry of Justice assessment paper: https://www.gov.uk/government/uploads/system/uploads/attachment_data/file/217392/peterborough-social-impact-bond-assessment.pdf.

38 UK Cabinet Office, April 2013: http://data.gov.uk/sib_knowledge_box/ministry-justice-offenders-released-peterborough-prison.

39 Ministry of Justice assessment paper: https://www.gov.uk/government/uploads/system/uploads/attachment_data/file/217392/peterborough-social-impact-bond-assessment.pdf.

40 UK Cabinet Office, April 2013: http://data.gov.uk/sib_knowledge_box/ministry-justice-offenders-released-peterborough-prison.

41 Growing the social investment market: 2013 progress update, HM government, pp. 5 and 12, https://www.gov.uk/government/uploads/system/uploads/attachment_data/file/205295/Social_Investment_Strategy_Update_2013.pdf.

42 J.P. Morgan, *Perspectives on Progress: The Impact Investor Survey, Global Impact Investing Network*, January 2013, p. 12, http://www.jpmorganchase.com/corporate/socialfinance/document/130107_Perspectives_on_Progress.pdf.

43 Developing a Mission-Related Investment Continuum: http://www.cfgreateratlanta.org/Repository/Files/MRI_snhuheroncasestudy.pdf.

44 *Philanthropy News Digest*: http://www.philanthropynewsdigest.org/commentary-and-opinion/it-s-the-year-of-impact-investing-what-does-that-mean-for-foundations.

45 Agua Natural en Red website (using Google Translate): http://www.agua-natural.com/ and Ignia website: http://www.ignia.com.mx/bop/portfolio-companies.php?cid=10.

46 GIIRS website: http://giirs.org/for-funds/pioneer.

47 J.P. Morgan Social Finance, "Insight into the Impact Investment Market: An In-Depth Analysis of Investor Perspectives and over 2,200 Transactions," Global Impact Investing Network, Social Finance Research, December 14, 2011, p. 6, http://www.thegiin.org/cgi-bin/iowa/download?row=334&field=gated_download_1.

48 "From the Margins to the Mainstream: Assessment of the Impact Investment Sector and Opportunities to Engage Mainstream Investors," World Economic Forum, September 2013, p. 27, http://www3.weforum.org/docs/WEF_II_ FromMarginsMainstream_Report_2013.pdf.

49 "Evolution of an Impact Portfolio: From Implementation to Results, Sonen Capital and the KL Felicitas Foundation," October 2013, http://www.sonencapital.com/ evolution-of-impact.php.

50 Investors' Circle website: http://www.investorscircle.net/accelsite/media/2244/IC%20 Portfolio%20and%20Exits.pdf.

51 Disclosure: Andrew Kassoy, one of the cofounders of B Lab, is author Margot Brandenburg's husband.

52 4-traders website: http://www.4-traders.com/UBS-AG-9365071/news/UBS-AG-UBS-launches-first-fund-for-Impact-Investing-17288728/.

53 IRIS website: http://iris.thegiin.org/.

54 B Lab: http://www.bcorporation.net/what-are-b-corps/legislation.

55 Impact Investing Collaborative, "The Revised Regulation 28 of the Pension Fund Act, South Africa Grow and Direct Private Capital," 2013, p. 2, http://iipcollaborative.org/ wp-content/uploads/media/Regulation-28_South-Africa_05-07-20132.pdf.

56 "OPIC Commits $87.5 Million to First Fund-of-Funds, Supporting Impact Investment," OPIC press release, May 14, 2012, http://www.opic.gov/press-releases/2012/opic-commits-875-million-first-fund-funds-supporting-impact-investment.

57 CDC Group website: http://www.cdcgroup.com/dfid-impact-fund.aspx.

58 Big Society Capital annual report, 2012, p. 4, http://www.bigsocietycapital.com/sites/ default/files/pdf/BSC_AR_AW_forwebsite.pdf.

59 Harvard University and the Rockefeller Foundation, "Impact at Scale: Policy Innovation for Institutional Investment with Social and Environmental Benefit, Pacific Community Ventures," February 2012, p. 16, http://hausercenter.org/iri/ wp-content/uploads/2010/05/FINAL_Impact-at-Scale_InSight_IRI_February-2012_ FULL-REPORT.pdf.

60 Quote sent by GIIN.

61 CFA Institute website: http://apic.cfainstitute.org/2012/03/19/rethinking-the-wealth-management-model-for-serving-asian-family-businesses/.

62 Ashish Karamchandani, Michael Kubzansky, and Paul Frandano, "Emerging Markets, Emerging Models: Market-Based Solutions to the Challenges of Global Poverty," Monitor Group, March 2009, p. 3, http://www.mim.monitor.com/downloads/emergingmarkets_full.pdf.

63 Karamchandani, Kubzansky, and Frandano, "Emerging Markets; Emerging Models," p. 14.

64 Indian Angel Network website: http://www.indianangelnetwork.com/companies.aspx.

65 Sarah Murray, "Living Space: Housing Solutions for Developing Nations," *Financial Times*, September 7, 2010; and the Acumen Fund: http://acumen.org/investment/saiban/.

66 Harvey Koh, Ashish Karamchandani, and Robert Katz, "From Blueprint to Scale: The Case for Philanthropy Impact Investing," Monitor Group, April 2012, http://www.mim.monitor.com/downloads/Blueprint_To_Scale/From%20Blueprint%20to%20Scale%20-%20Case%20for%20Philanthropy%20in%20Impact%20Investing_Full%20report.pdf.

67 Asia-Pacific Wealth Report 2011, Capgemini and Merrill Lynch Global Wealth Management: http://www.capgemini.com/resource-file-access/resource/pdf/Asia-Pacific_Wealth_Report_2011_____English_Version.pdf.

68 "Avantage Ventures Asia Pacific Impact Investment Report; Impact Investing in Asia: The Opportunities, The Challenges and Where It Is Headed": http://s3.amazonaws.com/zanran_storage/www.avantageventures.com/ContentPages/2500714485.pdf.

69 J.P. Morgan, "Perspectives on Progress: The Impact Investor Survey, Global Impact Investing Network," January 2013, p. 12, http://www.jpmorganchase.com/corporate/socialfinance/document/130107_Perspectives_on_Progress.pdf.

70 Philo Alto, "Impact Investing: Will Hype Stall Its Emergence as an Asset Class?" *Social Space*, 2012, p. 48: https://centres.smu.edu.sg/wp-content/uploads/2013/09/SocialSpace2012-PhiloAlto.pdf.

71 "Beyond the Margin: Redirecting Asia's Capitalism," Avatage Ventures, 2011, p. 6: http://www.global-inst.com/downloads/knowledge-tank/2011%20-%20AV%20-%20Beyond%20the%20Margin.pdf.

72 Margot Brandenburg and Paula Goldman, "Not London, Not New York: Emerging Centers of Gravity for Impact Investing Are in the Global South," *Huffington Post*, March 22, 2013, http://www.huffingtonpost.com/margot-brandenburg/impact-investing_b_2931818.html.

73 African Development Bank: http://www.afdb.org/en/annual-meetings/programme/demographic-dividend-or-time-bomb/.

74 Towers Watson, "Global Pension Fund Assets Survey, 2013": http://www.towerswatson.com/DownloadMedia.aspx?media=%7B5AC4BED2-A4F9-4C9E-AB9D-5087579BF96D%7D.

75 J.P. Morgan, "Perspectives on Progress: The Impact Investor Survey, Global Impact Investing Network," January 2013, p. 6, http://www.jpmorganchase.com/corporate/socialfinance/document/130107_Perspectives_on_Progress.pdf.

76 J.P. Morgan, "Perspectives on Progress: The Impact Investor Survey, Global Impact Investing Network," January 2013, p. 12, http://www.jpmorganchase.com/corporate/socialfinance/document/130107_Perspectives_on_Progress.pdf.

77 Monitor Inclusive Markets, "From Blueprint to Scale: The Case for Philanthropy in Impact Investing," April 2012, p. 14, http://www.mim.monitor.com/downloads/Blueprint_To_Scale/From%20Blueprint%20to%20Scale%20-%20Case%20for%20Philanthropy%20in%20Impact%20Investing_Full%20report.pdf.

78 Tina Rosenberg, "An Investment Strategy in the Human Interest," *New York Times*, June 19, 2013, http://opinionator.blogs.nytimes.com/2013/06/19/an-investment-strategy-in-the-human-interest/?_r=0.

79 Dalberg Global Development Advisors, "Impact Investing in West Africa," April 2011, p. 58, http://www.rockefellerfoundation.org/blog/impact-investing-west-africa.

80 Impact Investing Collaborative, "The Revised Regulation 28 of the Pension Fund Act, South Africa Grow and Direct Private Capital," 2013, p. 3, http://iipcollaborative.org/wp-content/uploads/media/Regulation-28_South-Africa_05-07-20132.pdf.

81 Jed Emerson, "Risk, Return and Impact, Understanding Diversification and Performance within an Impact Investing Portfolio," ImpactAssets brief, http://www.impactassets.org/files/downloads/ImpactAssets_IssueBriefs_2.pdf.

82 Lending Club statistics: https://www.lendingclub.com/info/statistics-performance.action.

83 Sarah Lynch, "SEC Releases 'Crowdfunding' Rule," Reuters, October 23, 2013, http://www.reuters.com/article/2013/10/23/us-sec-crowdfunding-idUSBRE99M03O20131023.

84 Elaine Moore, "Regulator Acts to Make Crowdfunding More Accessible," *Financial Times*, October 24, 2013.

85 "Gateways to Impact: Industry Survey of Financial Advisors on Sustainable and Impact Investing," June 2012, p. 4, http://www.gatewaystoimpact.org/images/gatewaystoimpact.pdf.

86 UNPRI: www.unpri.org.

87 Rockefeller Philanthropy Advisors, "Solutions for Impact Investors: From Strategy to Implementation," November 2009, http://rockpa.org/document.doc?id=15; and Rockefeller Philanthropy Advisors, "Impact Investing: An Introduction," Philanthropy Roadmap series, 2013, https://rockpa.org/document.doc?id=239.

Index

About the Authors

Judith Rodin is president of the Rockefeller Foundation, one of the world's leading philanthropic organizations. Since joining the Foundation in 2005, Dr. Rodin has recalibrated its focus to meet the challenges of the 21st century. Prior to the Rockefeller Foundation, she was the president of the University of Pennsylvania and provost of Yale University. Dr. Rodin is a graduate of the University of Pennsylvania and earned her PhD in psychology from Columbia University.

Margot Brandenburg was formerly senior associate director at the Rockefeller Foundation, where she managed its impact investing initiative. She is currently a fellow at the Nathan Cummings Foundation, where she is working on the launch of several social enterprise start-ups. She also chairs the board of Brooklyn Cooperative Credit Union and is adjunct faculty at New York University's Stern School of Business.

THE
R●CKEFELLER
FOUNDATION

About the Rockefeller Foundation

For more than 100 years, the Rockefeller Foundation's mission has been to promote the well-being of humanity throughout the world. Today, the Rockefeller Foundation pursues this mission through dual goals: advancing inclusive economies that expand opportunities for more broadly shared prosperity, and building resilience by helping people, communities, and institutions prepare for, withstand, and emerge stronger from acute shocks and chronic stresses. To achieve these goals, the Rockefeller Foundation works at the intersection of four focus areas (advance health, revalue ecosystems, secure livelihoods, and transform cities) to address the root causes of emerging challenges and create systemic change. Together with partners and grantees, the Rockefeller Foundation strives to catalyze and scale transformative innovations, create unlikely partnerships that span sectors, and take risks others cannot—or will not. To learn more, please visit www.rockefellerfoundation.org.

About Wharton Digital Press

Wharton Digital Press was established to inspire bold, insightful thinking within the global business community. In the tradition of The Wharton School of the University of Pennsylvania and its online business journal, *Knowledge@Wharton*, Wharton Digital Press uses innovative digital technologies to help managers meet the challenges of today and tomorrow.

As an entrepreneurial publisher, Wharton Digital Press delivers relevant, accessible, conceptually sound, and empirically based business knowledge to readers wherever and whenever they need it. Its format ranges from ebooks to print books available through print-on-demand technology. Directed to a general business audience, the Press's areas of interest include management and strategy, innovation and entrepreneurship, finance and investment, leadership, marketing, operations, human resources, social responsibility, and business-government relations.

wdp.wharton.upenn.edu

About The Wharton School

Founded in 1881 as the first collegiate business school, The Wharton School of the University of Pennsylvania is recognized globally for intellectual leadership and ongoing innovation across every major discipline of business education. With a broad global community and one of the most published business school faculties, Wharton creates ongoing economic and social value around the world. The School has 5,000 undergraduate, MBA, executive MBA, and doctoral students; more than 9,000 annual participants in executive education programs; and a powerful alumni network of 92,000 graduates.

www.wharton.upenn.edu

Made in the USA
Lexington, KY
15 March 2016